I'd Rather Be
Laughing

Finding Cheer in Every Circumstance

Marilyn Meberg

W PUBLISHING GROUP™

www.wpublishinggroup.com

A Division of Thomas Nelson, Inc.
www.ThomasNelson.com

Unless otherwise indicated, Scripture quotations used in this book are
from the Holy Bible, New International Version (NIV). Copyright © 1973,
1978, 1984 International Bible Society. Used by permission of Zondervan
Bible Publishers. Other Scripture references are from the following sources:

The King James Version (KJV) of the Bible.
The Living Bible (TLB), copyright © 1971 by Tyndale House Publishers,
Wheaton, Ill. Used by permission.
The New King James Version (NKJV), copyright © 1979, 1980, 1982,
1992, Thomas Nelson, Inc., Publisher.

Edited by Janet Kobobel Grant.

Some anecdotal characters in this volume are composites of actual
persons and events or are examples drawn from the author's experiences.
Details have been changed to protect identities.

"The First Time Ever I Saw Your Face" By Ewan MacColl. © Copyright
1962 (renewed) by Stormking Music, Inc. All Rights Reserved. Used by
permission.

"Temps Perdu" by Dorothy Parker, from *The Portable Dorothy Parker* by
Dorothy Parker. Introduction by Brendan Gill. Copyright 1928, renewed ©
1956 by Dorothy Parker. Used by permission of Viking Penguin, a division
of Penguin Books USA, Inc.

Library of Congress Cataloging-in-Publication Data

Meberg, Marilyn.
I'd rather be laughing : finding cheer in every circumstance / Marilyn Meberg.
p.   cm.
ISBN 0-8499-3989-5
1. Joy—Religious aspects.   2. Happiness—Religious aspects—
Christianity.   3. Cheerfulness.   4. Meberg, Marilyn.
I. Title.   II. Title: I would rather be laughing
BV4647.J68M43   1998   97-52653
242–dc21   CIP

Printed in the United States of America.
04 05 06 07 PHX 7

To my mother,
Elizabeth Downey Ricker,
who taught me
the joy of words,
the love of Jesus,
and the gift of laughter.

Contents

1
Giving Up Our Parking Spots

Do not grieve, for the joy of the LORD is your strength.
—Nehemiah 8:10

M arilyn, I've just had a thought worthy of deep con-templation!"

I looked over at my husband, Ken, lying casually on the couch with his legs thrown over the back cushions, maga-zine temporarily resting on his chest, and his eyes fixed warmly on mine. I noted a familiar twinkle that usually preceded a statement I didn't want to miss.

"Okay, Babe, what's your thought?"

"Well, simply put, if no one ever died, it would become increasingly difficult to find a place to park."

I reacted first with incredulity, followed by a giggle that worked its way into a major guffaw. Ken's off-the-wall humor frequently produced that sequence of responses in me. It was his quirky ability to see the funny side of life that first drew me to him. (He was cute too.)

A few minutes later, as I made a pretense of returning to my book, I pondered Ken's indomitable spirit. Thirteen months prior to this crazy statement, he had been diag-nosed with pancreatic cancer and given four to six months to live. Instead, he lived fourteen months. The way he met the challenges of those last months inspired me and continues to do so even now.

It never ceases to amaze me what load-lifters cheer and humor are.

Through it all—the chemo, the radiation, the nausea, and even those moments of fear—Ken's humor prevailed. In fact, on the human level, his humor lightened many heavy moments. And that is what we'll explore together in this book: how we can be of good cheer when life hands us bad stuff. We can choose to see amusing moments in the midst of confusing and dark times. That choice does not make the confusing and dark times disappear, but it strengthens us as well as lightens our load so that we are more capable of coping. It never ceases to amaze me what load-lifters cheer and humor are. And Ken was very good at this cheerful business.

Shortly after he was due to give up his earthly parking space, Ken began to rally instead. He regained some of the one hundred pounds he had lost as well as some of his stamina. We were thrilled and even dared to believe he had been healed. We wanted to do something as a family to celebrate. So we elected to take a Caribbean cruise together and had a fabulously memorable time. On that cruise, Ken's zany humor was witnessed over and over, not only by us, but also by others on board.

Now I need to warn you that both Ken and I always have been responsive to what can be described as "dark humor." Admittedly, it can be off-putting to many, and should you fall into that category, you may find this anecdote more troublesome than funny. But for Ken it seemed to maintain his balance, and I must admit, it did mine as well.

Because Ken had lost so much weight, he was constantly hungry. So he was thrilled to learn that not only were the usual three meals a day served on the ship but also scores of food opportunities in between. The first night he discovered the midnight buffet, he enthusiastically grabbed a plate and cut to the front of the line. Turning to the people he had edged out, he said, "Excuse me, I hope you don't mind my cutting in, but you see, I'm scheduled to die before long, and I hate to leave hungry."

Because Ken looked as if he truly could fade away any moment, people fell back and with genuine concern deferred to him, urging him to please go ahead and take his time (fearing he had none). Ken was so utterly charming and winsome it wasn't long before he made scores of friends, all of whom encouraged him to take cuts in the serving lines and brought him food even when he wasn't hungry. In time, that food was accompanied with broad smiles and comments like, "Glad to see you're still around. How about a brownie?"

On the cruise's final night, the tuxedoed waiters concluded the evening meal by emerging from the kitchen in single file, each holding aloft in his right hand a lighted baked Alaska. As they festively wound their way through the dining room, Ken stepped into the line holding his empty palm skyward. Our waiter placed his baked Alaska onto Ken's hand, and he continued in the procession instead of the waiter. When his food buddies saw him, they clapped, cheered, and chanted, "Eat it all, Ken!"

Later that night in our cabin bed, Ken was chuckling softly in the dark. I asked him what was funny, and he said, "I was just thanking God I can still laugh."

> *I was just thanking God I can still laugh.*

Laughter Medicine

When I talk about Ken's prevailing sense of humor in the midst of one of life's greatest extremities, I want to point out that he was taking his medicine. Proverbs 17:22 states, "A cheerful heart is good medicine, but a crushed spirit dries up the bones."

He was taking the laughter medicine God prescribes for all His children. We need a prescription most when we're sick . . . when we're in need . . . when we feel weak. A prescription does us no good if we don't take what is prescribed. Ken chose to take what was prescribed by his Divine Physician. The benefits to his body, soul, and spirit were enormous.

Taking his medicine didn't mean he ignored the anguishing reality of his diagnosis or that he lived in a La-La Land of denial. We both had many excruciating emotions to deal with, but occasional doses of laughter medicine in the midst of all that earthquake-shaking of the soul was sustaining to us both and certainly was an antidote for dry bones.

A Deathbed Plan for Laughter

My all-time favorite memory of Ken's humor, as well as what proved to be medicine for us both, requires me to first give you a bit of history, and that history has to do with my hair. My hair became noticeably gray by the time I was sixteen. I started to color it at age twenty-seven. By age forty I wondered if I should just show my age and not color it anymore. Possibly being forty warranted gray hair. I asked Ken for his opinion. He strongly encouraged me to continue coloring. At age forty-five, I consulted him again about this issue, and he continued to have the same strong response.

However, when I hit fifty, it seemed to me some sort of half-century commemoration was in order. I would let my hair grow out. Also, I had become increasingly concerned about the widely published carcinogen potential in hair color. Ken adamantly maintained I did not need to go public with my hair.

A couple of weeks before Ken died, I sat down next to him and told him I needed to discuss a weighty issue. He became very solicitous, thinking I had finally decided to talk about business stuff—like insurance forms, paying the mortgage, etc. In other words, practical realities. (Such topics tended to put me in a mild coma no matter what the circumstances.) The conversation went something like this:

"Babe, you know you are going to be leaving me soon."

"Yes."

"Well, I really need to talk to you about my hair."

"Your *hair?*"

"Yes, my hair. You know, there really is no point in my

continuing to color it if you're not here. I think I'll just let it go."

"You're serious, aren't you, Marilyn? I can't believe it. You really are going to do it; I can tell."

He looked at me for a few long seconds, and then, with that familiar twinkle, he said, "Okay, you go ahead with that plan, but I'd like to suggest you do it in a way that will give you mileage."

"Mileage? Mileage for what?"

"Now bear with me. How long do you figure it will take to grow out?"

"I have no idea. . . . I don't know what's under there."

"Well, okay, let's assume three months. Here's how you'll get mileage. After I'm gone, don't go out. Don't go out until your hair has grown out. When *it's* out, you go out."

"Babe, I'm sorry, but I don't get it. How on earth do I get mileage out of that plan?"

"Think about it. You'll probably be totally white-headed. No one will have seen you since the funeral. When you appear in public with white hair, everyone will be overcome with compassion for you. They will say things like, 'Have you seen Marilyn? Oh, bless her heart. She's turned totally white since Ken died. They were so close, you know.' People will take you to dinner or the movies or both. You should be able to work that one at least a year."

Once again I went through the three steps of incredulity, giggling, and finally guffawing. Who but Ken Meberg could come up with a deathbed plan that would ensure an occasional meal for his white-haired widow?

Almost Worth the Price

The circumstances we experience in life are frequently not a matter of choice, but the attitudes we have toward those circumstances are *always* a matter of choice. The Pakistani people have a saying that, when you find yourself in a difficult situation, you either become an egg or a potato. An egg thrust into hot water turns hard. A potato becomes soft.

What seemed to us a premature as well as unwelcome prognosis of death was a circumstance about which Ken would have to make a choice. He could become hard, impenetrable, bitter and unapproachable. Or he could choose to be soft, pliable, and open to whatever God had for him during the remainder of his life.

Ken obviously chose the latter, and as a result, he developed a vast network of other cancer patients, all of whom called him. Sometimes they phoned for specific counsel but more often simply to receive his warm and caring encouragement. Many times I would hear Ken explain the plan of salvation to those who were close to dying and felt frightened and unsure of eternity.

One particularly memorable man was from Michigan. He was angry and bitter about the "hand that had been dealt him." He and Ken were the same age, and the man couldn't understand Ken's faith or his lack of anger. This dear gentleman sometimes called several times a day and would talk for more than an hour about his feelings and his bitterness. Finally, shortly before the man died, I heard Ken praying with him over the phone to receive Christ.

That was a wonderfully sweet and tender experience for Ken. "Almost worth the price of my cancer," he said to me.

Cheerful Despite the Death Penalty

In spite of these meaningful moments of encouragement and ministering to others, I found myself then and even now hating the fact that cancer and death are a part of life. Of all the hurts we can experience, none is as wrenching as a loved one's death. It's an enormous assault to the soul and spirit. I think to deal fully with it in our minds as well as in our souls we need to understand its origins.

We'll need to venture back to the Garden of Eden. Remember that God gave Adam very clear instructions on how to avoid death. In Genesis 2:16–17, He said, "You are free to eat from any tree in the garden; but you must not eat from the tree of the knowledge of good and evil, for when you eat of it you will surely die."

But Adam disobeyed and ate anyway.

The comfort and point of cheer in all this is that God provides for us an eternity with Him in spite of the death penalty. Paul, in Romans 5:15–16, clearly states why we can be of good cheer. "For this one man, Adam, brought death to many through his *sin*. But this one man, Jesus Christ, brought forgiveness to many through God's *mercy*. Adam's *one* sin brought the penalty of death to many, while Christ freely takes away *many* sins and gives glorious life instead" (TLB).

We read in Romans 5:18–19: "Yes, Adam's *sin* brought *punishment* to all, but Christ's *righteousness* makes men *right* with God, so that they can live. Adam caused many to be sinners because he *disobeyed* God, and Christ caused many to be made acceptable to God because he *obeyed*" (TLB).

Concluding now with Romans 5:21: "Before, sin ruled over all men and brought them to death, but now God's kindness rules instead, giving us right standing with God and resulting in eternal life through Jesus Christ our Lord" (TLB).

> *God provides for us an eternity with Him in spite of the death penalty.*

Well now, that feels a lot better, doesn't it? I have every reason to dislike, even hate, disease and death. They are enemies of the soul and spirit born of disobedience and sin. But even in that we can be of good cheer, because on the cross Christ overcame the cost of Adam's sin and in so doing ensured a place for each of us in heaven for all eternity.

Laughter in the Cemetery

Of course, some of us manage to add to others' cheer by how we exit from life. At a conference I met a dear little lady who was ninety-one years old. She possessed the snappiest blue eyes I'd ever seen. She assured me that being of good cheer had always been her theology as well as philosophy, and she mentioned that she knew beyond a shadow of a doubt that her fun-loving husband, whom she had recently buried, was luxuriating in heaven even as we spoke.

"But," she said, "I also know he's still laughing about his burial service."

Then she sidled in closer to me and said, "Bet you'd like to know what I'm talking about, wouldn't you?"

Of course I did!

She told me her husband, George, was an avid golfer and that he had wanted to be buried in the cemetery adjoining his favorite golf course. Years ago he had purchased a hilltop plot to ensure his preference.

At some point prior to the burial service, the wheels on the casket cart slipped their moorings, and the cart began to roll away from the burial site. It quickly gained momentum until it was flying down the hill.

She told me everyone was so shocked, the gathering group just stared in stunned disbelief until, she said, "I fell back into the chair behind me and just roared with laughter. I couldn't stop laughing until the cart hit a tree and came to a stop. In fact, everyone got so giggly we never did quite regain our composure, even after the grave people managed to push George back up the hill."

I must admit I was a bit horrified as this was being described to me, but my little friend said, "You know, Marilyn, I just know George would have loved that. He loved to laugh, and I'm sure he would have preferred us to laugh than to cry. It'd be just like him to pay the mortician to ensure that the casket cart would cut loose at the right time."

As I gave her a hug and thanked her for her story, she said, "By the way, my plot is on the hill next to George's. Think there's any chance when my day comes that I too will take a flying leap?"

Looking into her sparkling eyes, I told her I'd love to be there just in case.

The Right Time to Die

Now before we put this chapter to rest, I'd like to discuss a couple of other issues associated with death. One of them is the idea of premature death. Because Ken was fifty-two when he died, I have often thought and even said his death was premature. Actually, as you probably already know, that is an unbiblical concept. There is no such thing as premature death. Job 14:5 states, "Man's days are determined; you have decreed the number of his months and have set limits he cannot exceed."

And Psalm 139:16 says, "All the days ordained for me were written in your book before one of them came to be."

I find that realization comforting. In fact, it could be a cheer-up thought. To recognize God's sovereign determining of the number of days each of us is to have on earth relieves me of nagging questions like, "If I had just done this, eaten that, not eaten that, stayed home, not stayed home . . .".

This is not some kind of Christian fatalism in which we assume it doesn't matter if we take health and safety precautions. On the contrary, Scripture says our bodies are the temples of the Holy Spirit, and we must respect them as well as do our part in preserving them. But tension is released in me as I remember that the number of my days is in His hands and not mine.

Based on Scripture, then, I can say that God did not intend for Ken to stay on earth one day longer than he did. Based on Scripture, he did not die prematurely. He was ushered into God's presence at exactly the time God had chosen for him.

Another dimension of premature death has been an encouragement to my heart. That is concerning a baby girl we had named Joani, who was born with spina bifida and died when she was fifteen days old. In my humanness, I have felt I certainly could say she died prematurely. But according to Scripture I still can't use that phrase though the days ordained for her were so few.

Baby Joani's death left a hole in my soul that will never fully be filled in, but I have basically come to terms with the idea that her short life on earth was just that: short. What encourages me is the realization that if God, through my union with Ken, had not created her, she simply would not be at all. Because I've never known her, even held her, it sometimes feels as if she never was. But the reality is, she was and continues to be because God chose to create her. In addition to that, she is a living, loving, active being—a fully realized entity who lives in heaven. She simply beat me home. For that matter, so did her daddy.

One last thought on premature death. I don't know anyone I have loved who did not seem to have died prematurely. I know it's never premature from God's perspective, but from my human, emotional perspective, it still feels premature. For instance, my mother died at seventy-six. That was too soon. I wasn't ready for her to go. My father died at seventy-eight; that also was too soon. You see, we don't ever want to lose our connection with those we love.

We weren't created for disconnectedness; we were created for unbroken continuity. We lost that in Eden. In other words, no matter how young or how old our loved one is, it goes against that original imprint in our souls to have those loving ties severed. We were created for unending, continuous fellowship with each other and with Him.

Choose Life

What I have suggested in this chapter is that death, despite its inevitability, need not make me feel powerless. Those options have to do with my attitudes and even my willingness to take my medicine. I can choose to become hard, cynical, and bitter, or I can choose to be softened, responsive, and productive. I can allow the light of His life and love to shine through me, or I can turn away and sit in the murky stillness of my disillusionment. Because I cannot bear that, because His love is too real to me to turn from, I choose the attitude expressed in Deuteronomy 30:19–20: "I have set before you life and death, blessings and curses. Now choose life, so that you and your children may live and that you may love the LORD your God, listen to His voice, and hold fast to him. For the LORD is your life."

In upcoming chapters we'll look at other factors that deplete us of cheer. And we'll examine ways we can reinsert humor and joy into our lives even though those factors can't be changed. Some of the "stuff" of life is mundane and draining while other parts of life are enormous and hard. Whatever the size of the difficulty, cheer is waiting to be discovered—sometimes unexpectedly, like a chocolate chip in the raisin bran.

2
How Things Don't Work

Rejoice before the LORD your God in everything you put your hand to.

—Deuteronomy 12:18

My non-theological definition of hell is a place full of computers, sewing machines, and high-heeled shoes. It is also full of things that don't work. In all reality, that's not hell. That's earth! I'm sure hell has a few more odious things like math stuff, tax forms, and endless platters of liver and onions thrown in as well.

Did you ever stop to wonder about all the things in your life that don't work or work only occasionally and on their own terms? Now, by "things" I mean, in the language of Webster's dictionary, "an article, device, etc. used for some purpose." You probably have not given it a lot of thought because these pesky thing-breakdowns seem a fact of life; so we do the best we can to accommodate them without losing our cool or our minds.

Riding the Washer, Dodging the Toast

For example, my washing machine immediately comes to my mind as a thing that chooses to work on its own terms.

This less-than-perfect appliance is, to use the language of the politically correct, balance challenged. The two little screw-like doodads on which her front rests are too high. I don't know why or when this happened, but I suspect it was sometime in the night. At any rate, when she goes into her spin cycle, she rocks and knocks wildly about, threatening to burst through the laundry room door and escape out into the neighborhood. One day, in an effort to restore balance to these wild gyrations, I lay over the machine and held on for dear life. I was hoping the weight of my body would counterbalance something or other.

Since I'm prone to motion sickness, I became increasingly nauseous until the machine finally lurched into her soak cycle. Since nausea is one of my most hated feelings, I was pleased to discover that if I simply sat on the machine it was just as effective as lying on it. And sitting did not nauseate me. In fact, I could even read a magazine as long as I extended my arms from my body to avoid movement. Actually, I've become so skilled at mounting up and riding out the spin cycle I'm getting quite a bit of reading done.

Years ago, we had a straight-from-post-Eden toaster that used to test my patience every morning from 7:00 to 7:15. I never could quite figure out her pattern because it varied from day to day. Some mornings she would fling out the toast with such ill-placed abandon the children had to position themselves in various parts of the kitchen and then leap or stretch to catch breakfast. Other mornings the toast would laboriously creep up to the level of near visibility and, while peeking out at us, slowly burn to death. For some reason we were reluctant to replace that toaster; something about her colorful unpredictability kept us amused as well as strangely empathic.

A Light unto the Bike Path

Yesterday, Patsy Clairmont, who is part of our Joyful Journey team of speakers, pedaled her brand-new bicycle over to my condo for the enthusiastic appraisal she knew she would receive. (Incidentally, a few months ago, Les and Patsy were feeling the effects of their cold Michigan winter. Luci Swindoll, who is also part of the Joyful Journey group, and I convinced Patsy and Les to try living in our California desert complex for a few weeks just to soak up the winter sunshine. They loved it so much, they bought my former condo and moved in immediately. Because they are only one block from me and two blocks from Luci you can imagine the fun we are having as we run in and out of each other's homes leaving a trail of statements like, "Don't you dare tell that!" and "For sure you can't write about *that!*")

Now, back to Patsy's new bike. In addition to wanting to show off her recently acquired toy, she also wanted to put batteries in the front and back light fixtures so she could prowl around at night with fewer chances of running into parked cars. (However, with Patsy, those kinds of possibilities can never be totally eliminated.) Les was busy putting together Malibu lights for the side yard, and she hated to bother him with a small job like bike lights.

Pat Wenger, another wonderful friend who lives three

doors down from Luci, was at my house attempting to cajole a more civil and cooperative spirit from my computer (a machine I loathe and am convinced knows nothing of redemption, nor will it ever). While Pat tried every tactic she could think of to tame my computer, I went outside with the intention of helping Patsy equip her bike with battery-powered lights.

It never occurred to me that battery-installing would be a task beyond my technological abilities. After all, I can crumble in defeat before my computer and still preserve some shred of self-respect simply because I know there's a whole community of people who are overwhelmed and intimidated by their computers out there. But I didn't know *anyone* who couldn't open the plastic dome that houses the bike lights and slip in a battery.

Patsy held the bike, and I tugged, pushed, shoved, and ultimately began muttering about the thoughtlessness of Adam and Eve in introducing sinful things—like contrary bike lights—into the world. The little dome refused to open or cooperate in any way. Pat, who can fix anything (we in the neighborhood call her Mrs. Goodwrench), came confidently to the rescue. Thirty minutes later I suggested we buy a ten-pound hammer. I figured I could use it as a means of communicating with my computer after we finished with the bike.

Since we met with no success, Patsy made her uncertain way home in the dark, and I again took up my gripe about Adam and Eve. (Les put her lights in the next morning in a matter of moments.)

Questions from the Demon

If you have the stamina for it, let me take you from Patsy's bicycle lights to my computer. For at least a year, I steadfastly refused to entertain the notion of owning a computer. I could usually get people to quit talking to me about it by simply saying I didn't trust anything with moving parts unless it was human. By the time they figured out that didn't make a lot of sense, I would have slipped away, avoiding the subject.

When I retired my counseling practice, moved to the desert, and signed a two-book contract with W Publishing Group, it seemed clear to those who take a proprietary interest in my well-being that a computer would be a necessity. The prevailing logic was, "Marilyn, once you get the hang of it, and you will very soon, you will be stunned at the amount of time saved by using a computer for your writing."

I have long harbored the suspicion that I could not sleep in a place that also housed a computer. However, when my son, Jeff, and his wife, Carla, began to talk about the advantages of a computer for me, I started to listen. I suppose the clincher was the fact that Carla and I could do battle for who qualifies as more technologically challenged. If Carla could master a computer, then surely there was hope for me.

Under the inspiration of that realization and with the persistently kind advice of many, Pat Wenger volunteered to buy a laptop computer for me. The laptop came equipped to do all I needed and more, should I choose.

I have long harbored the suspicion that I could not sleep in a place that also housed a computer. Pat made the purchase because I couldn't imagine being in the same room with a bunch of computers, let alone a whole store full of electronic gadgets. Nor would I have the foggiest notion of what questions to ask. Pat feared I might in all innocence and incompetence come home with a digital machine to measure blood pressure.

I will spare you the details of the hours and even days I have lost in my efforts to save time by using a computer, but I would like to say that computers are utterly inexplicable to me. Not only that, but they also have an attitude. At least mine does! For instance, something as simple as closing out a program and shutting down the computer sends the little demonic person who scowlingly sits inside the machine day and night into parental mode. A question flashes on the screen: "Are you sure you want to shut down your machine?" Until the question was asked, I was quite certain I wanted to shut it down, but with those bold words glaring at me, I hesitate. Maybe I was wrong. Does the little machine person know something I don't? Will something irreparable happen if it shuts down? Not wanting to appear uncertain, I click yes. But my self-confidence is undermined, and I wait nervously for the whole thing to explode all over my lap.

Another equally unsettling question the little demonic machine person loves to flash on the screen is, "Are you sure you want to do that?" I hate that because I'm not *sure* about anything. I'd like to say, "Don't ask," but I'm too intimidated. Instead, I find myself talking aloud to the screen in an effort to justify my thinking.

The most judgmental action the computer has ever taken with me occurred when, in utter disgust and frustration, I typed in an accusatory word that I must admit I would not use in polite society. However, I felt it was appropriate for the demonic little person who had been second-guessing, bossing, and not cooperating with me all morning. The minute I typed in my retort, the screen went blank, but not before telling me it would not tolerate my word.

As long as I'm venting, let me say I find computer terminology utterly illogical. For instance, why on earth is a paper copy called "hard copy"? It isn't hard at all. On the other hand a "floppy disk" is as unpliable as the character living in my computer. Why not call a paper copy "floppy" and a disk "hard"? Now isn't that logical?

I had the audacity to express these thoughts one evening to a group of computer literates (one of my more boring evenings) and received lofty, patronizing statements like, "It's really not all that difficult."

As long as we're talking computer absurdities, can anyone tell me why on earth the pointer is called a mouse? For goodness sake, a mouse is a rodent! I can't imagine anything more repellent than having daily hand contact with something called a mouse. If we have to have an image of something small and furry that illogically represents a pointer, why not call it a canary? At least they're appealing. Good grief! I've worked myself up to needing that blood-pressure machine I wasn't allowed to buy.

Life's Little Cheer Depleters

As you well know, scores of other things in life don't work in addition to washing machines, bike lights, toasters, and computers. What about those shopping carts whose left wheels go in the opposite direction of their right wheels, causing you to lurch dangerously up and down the aisles, never sure you won't find yourself suddenly pitched into the frozen food case? Or how about those other maddening items that require batteries? One item requires a double A but another will only stare blankly at you if you don't feed it a triple A.

But the most maddening batteries to me are those teensy, flat, disc-like ones that go into watches, baby calculators, auto alarm beepers, and who knows what else. At times the discarded ones have ridden around in the depths of my purse for months, simply because I can't find them to buy a matching replacement. It would require a telescope to pull them into my range of vision.

I can't imagine anything more repellent than having daily hand contact with something called a mouse.

These are small tests of our fortitude, but they, too, come under the banner of cheer depleters, as do ants in the kitchen and flies on the patio. Or how about the need to keep gas in the car? I hate that. It annoys me to have to stop wherever I'm going, pull up to the pump, and wait until my car gets her fill of octane so I can then continue on my way.

Being interrupted could (and often does) become a cheer depleter for me. For instance, just making time for a haircut can get on my nerves. "So what's the deal?" I ask my silver locks. "You were just cut. Why are you once again hanging on with such weight I need a neck brace to keep my head up!"

I think it's simple maintenance that can become so annoying. Once the house is tidy, vacuumed, dusted, etc., why can't it just stay that way? But it never does. Even if I were to sit unmoving in the middle of the floor for several weeks so as to avoid creating clutter, there still is that insidious dust that will creep in and settle down all around me.

The Privilege of Partnering with God

Life is filled with annoying little cheer depleters. I have often pondered how many of these little imperfections to bring to God's attention and how many to simply pass off. Will my cheer increase if I talk to God about the things that don't work?

For instance, does it make sense to ask God for a sunny day with no smog because Aunt Wilda is coming from Toronto, and I want it to be nice for her? Is it reasonable as I walk into the office supply store to ask God to help me find the fax machine paper that doesn't curl up like a scroll the minute it exits my machine? Does it make sense to pray that my newspaper be delivered a bit early so I can take it with me on my morning flight since I forgot to put it on vacation hold? To what degree is God involved in these daily issues?

My friend Ney Bailey has a faith I respect enormously. She is so practical in her faith she prays about everything.

She even claims God's intervention in the provision of parking spaces. We have debated this question for years. It has always seemed to me that I trivialize my relationship with God by throwing everything to Him as if He had not provided me with sufficient brain power to make decisions about the various trivia of life. (As I typed that statement, my computer just let out a derisive "Ha!" . . . cheeky machine. Or maybe it was a beep; could my battery be running low?) Yet I know God invites us to take all our concerns to Him. He never qualifies those concerns as big ones or little ones. His Word says every concern of ours is a concern of His.

I have assumed His attitude toward us is one of immense care. But that doesn't mean I should toss daily trivia to Him, does it? The trouble with my thinking is I don't know at what point of my "carings" to bring God into the picture. What constitutes the cutoff point between big and small?

Not long ago I had lunch with Luci Swindoll and her brother Orville. He had come to California to install some new and complex computer equipment for Luci. As we were lunching, I gave my personal, as well as unsolicited, testimony about computers. That led to a discussion of prayer and the degree to which we pull God into our various small concerns. I asked Orville for his view.

He said, "You know, Marilyn, I pray about everything. Absolutely everything. For me, it is not so much the items I want Him to take note of as it is my desire to have unbroken communication with Him. I just want Him in on everything! Talking to Him causes me to sense our partnership."

The simple profundity of his comments caused this age-old issue finally to recede for me. I think one of my mental and spiritual hang-ups has been that, because of the fallout from the Fall, I've assumed I have to muck my own way through certain things; it's part of the package. I've never assumed God's indifference but have questioned my own need to use my head. Now I see the notion

It is not so much the items I want Him to take note of as it is my desire to have unbroken communication with Him.

of bringing God into everything has nothing to do with trivializing Him; it has to do with the privilege of partnering with Him. When I include God on my wild washing-machine rides and as I mentally travel in circles with my computer and its attitude, I'm cheered by His companionship and the knowledge that I'm in partnership with Him.

Why don't you give it a try? Today as you encounter things that don't work, include God in the aftermath of machinery gone haywire. It cheers me up just to think about that!

I'm going to do more partnering, and I'm going to start right now.

Lord, help me to understand why when I hit the tab button on my computer, all the words race toward the right-hand side of the screen, leap off, and go tearing down the hall. Amen.

3
Standard Equipment: A Zippered Heart

*Only be careful, and watch yourselves closely so that you do
not forget the things your eyes have seen or let them slip from
your heart as long as you live. Teach them to your children
and to their children after them.*

—Deuteronomy 4:9

I can just imagine my twenty-one-month-old grandson's
thoughts during our playtime in the park:

*It's hard enough when some little blonde girl shorter than
you takes your swing just seconds before you can manage
to toddle over to grab it first. And it certainly isn't easy to
have some bigger boy push you out of the slide line and
then call you "baby" just 'cause you whimpered. Worse
yet, a mother is having a private birthday party for some
little kid with too much hair and funny-looking red pants,
but no other people at the playground get to join in. It
looked like a pretty good party too, because the chocolate
on the cake wasn't too dark or too light. I could see my
grandma's eyes light up when she saw the cake, but she
still kept walking straight ahead with me in her arms.*

Life got better, though, 'cause when my grandma was

shackling me in the car seat she said we would get a Happy Meal at McDonald's, and I could even have some sips of her Coke. That made me smile really big. While we were driving, Grandma told me life has a lot of challenges but it also has a lot of Happy Meals too. Whatever all that means.

I can tell she really loves me, but she still won't let me get into her purse. I gotta admit, it makes me wonder if she has something to hide!

It's true; I don't let little Ian in my purse, because I learned some months ago his idea of lipstick use does not coincide with mine, and he has yet to develop a spirit of negotiation. This little guy, however, has my heartfelt admiration, because he is working through some losses in his baby life. And he is figuring out how to be cheerful despite those losses. That's why I figured he needed to know that Happy Meals are a part of life too.

Growing through the Losses

Ian's mama, my daughter, Beth, was hospitalized last spring because her body was threatening to deliver little three-pound Alec seven weeks early. What her doctor as well as all of us feared did not happen, but she had to rest in bed so that Alec stayed put and arrived on schedule in the middle of May. When Beth was put on "bed rest," I flew up immediately to be chief cook, bottle washer, and wisdom-dispensing baby-sitter.

What impressed me about Ian's resiliency and ability to

cheerfully absorb losses was that Beth's night in the hospital was the first time he had ever been separated from her for more than a few hours. In addition to that, because nursing Ian brings on contractions, Beth had to abruptly give up breast-feeding.

Not only did Ian manage the two-day, one-night hospitalization with surprising equanimity, he also cooperated fully with the loss of "nummies," which we were sure would trouble him enormously. Though he did whimper a time or two the first day, something in him resolved it all, and he took comfort from an occasional bottle. With a quick toss of his head, he would take a swig, gulp it down loudly, slam down the bottle, and go about his business with manly aplomb.

I was pleased to see Ian's ability to absorb these early-in-life losses, because as a grandma, I don't want his little soul to be anguished. But, in addition to that, I know that life will not always hand Ian Happy Meals. He doesn't fully know this yet, but thanks to the Fall, loss is a major theme in life. There will be more lost swings, slides, and birthday cakes with perfect-looking chocolate. He will one day, years from now, experience separation from people he has grown to love. He will experience some losses in his romantic hopes and dreams and perhaps periodic losses in his aspirations for a certain profession or a specific position within that profession. One day he will, as his grandma is now, have to deal with the loss of his younger self and younger body. And he too will one day face the loss of his children, who will grow up and become independent and self-sufficient.

But, of course, hidden in each loss lies the potential for enormous gain. What God gives when life takes is a source of hope, optimism, and cheerfulness for all of us. With an attitude of acceptance and teachability, our losses can enrich and enlarge our interior being, which can, in turn, help us never to lose sight of the Happy Meal just around the corner.

Loving and Letting Go

A specific loss that has enlarged my interior landscape regards my daughter, Beth. I have not liked this loss, nor would I have chosen it. But God has shown Himself to be a God of incredible style and, as always, very near to me when I needed Him to scoot in close.

When Joani died, Ken and I felt we would just settle down and not have more children. Our little boy, Jeff, was a source of incredible joy, and because of the genetic counseling we received, it seemed risky to

What God gives when life takes is a source of hope, optimism, and cheerfulness for all of us.

have another child. With the passing of time, however, we began to long for a baby girl.

Years earlier, Ken and I had determined on our second date that we each wanted two children, a boy and a girl, and that whomever we might marry, we hoped that person would be of the same mind. (I took careful note of that conversation, and we later laughed about it as it became obvious we would be each other's "whomever.")

With the desire growing in each of us for that baby girl we had talked about early in our courtship, we were thrilled with our decision to adopt. We began the year-long process of applying, being found acceptable, and then being told "our" baby would be born sometime in August. The agency had matched us up with a young couple who were similar to us in interests, abilities, and values. We were ecstatic.

On August 24, 1967, I was buried up to my elbows in dirt. (Not in my house but in my garden. Nothing soothes my soul as much as digging in the dirt, planting and mulching.) As I was puttering happily about, the phone rang, and our social worker from the adoption agency said, "Well, Marilyn, you and Ken had a baby girl eight days ago! She has red hair, a cherubic little face, and the foster mother says she loves music. How would you all like to come to the agency tomorrow to pick her up?"

What a way to have a baby! No pain, no stitches, no hospital; only sweet-smelling dirt and flowers. I called Ken immediately and told him we had just had a baby. He let out a whoop and said he was coming right home. I told him we wouldn't pick her up until tomorrow and that he didn't need to come home yet. His comment was, "I have to fill the car with gas, and you have to fill the bottles with milk!"

With that celebratory statement, he let out another whoop and hung up. I dashed outside and threw a little dirt into the air, let out a few whoops of my own, and then tore down the street to pull Jeff away from his little buddies for a minute to tell him he had just become a big brother.

The next day, three-year-old Jeff, Ken, and I made our eager way to Whittier, California, where baby Elizabeth awaited our arrival. We were ushered into a room where, against the opposite wall, was a little pink bassinet. As we made the short but interminable walk across the floor to the bassinet, I was acutely aware that within moments I would scoop up a tiny life that would forever change ours. And indeed she did.

We were advised by the agency to use the word *adoption* frequently and in an atmosphere of love. That hopefully would ensure a warm and positive response from Beth; so, of course, we conscientiously used the word in that context.

> *Within moments I would scoop up a tiny life that would forever change ours. And indeed she did.*

The counsel was wise, because had we not been so advised, we would probably not have thought to employ such a plan. We kept forgetting she was adopted.

We also explained to her, long before she could fully understand, that God had created her specifically for our family. In His sovereign design (Beth's eyes always glazed over at that point), He had chosen Jeff to be her big brother, Ken to be her daddy, and me to be her mommy. God had *chosen* her for us and chosen us for her.

Apparently, she absorbed more of the explanation than I thought, because some years later (when Beth was four and Jeff was seven) Jeff came running into the house and with obvious agitation said to me, "Mama, did you get stuck with me?"

I couldn't imagine what had prompted the question, but I assured him that of course we didn't get stuck with him. Why did he ask?

"Well, Beth said she got *chose* but that you got *stuck* with me!"

We realized then that perhaps we had given Beth greater confidence about her origins than we had Jeff. So I again launched into the grand theology of God's sovereign design for our family only to watch Jeff make a hasty retreat back into the yard saying, "Okay, okay, Mama. Thanks. I'm going now."

When Beth was in high school, we asked her several times if she had any curiosity about her birth parents, and we told her if she did we wanted her to know she could talk about it with us. We had long ago told her the little we knew, which was that both the mother and father were very young, from the Chicago area, and wanted their baby to be raised in a Christian home. Beth always said she didn't need to know any more and that she felt perfectly free to talk to us should she want to.

She went off to Westmont College in Santa Barbara and decided to major in psychology. During the Thanksgiving vacation of Beth's junior year, she told us a number of students in her psych major were adopted and that they wanted to know more of their origins. She told us that for several years a curiosity as well as a restlessness had been growing within her and that now she too wanted to know more.

We quickly assured her that she should investigate if she wanted to and if in any way we could be of assistance, we were eager to do what we could. That was the politically correct answer to give, but the truth was that we both felt as if we had been hit in the stomach with a sledgehammer.

Shortly after this conversation, however, Ken's cancer diagnosis came in, and the search was shelved as we all banded together to be there for Ken as well as for each other. Ken died May 5, 1990; Jeff was married one month later; and during the week following Jeff's wedding, Beth asked how I would feel if she resumed her search. The sledgehammer swung even harder this time.

For years I have kept in reserve a mental image that I call forth in those moments when the sledgehammer strikes or whenever I need help keeping my thinking straight and my behavior in line. As I feel myself struggling to cope with unexpected trials, I see my heart as having, as part of its standard equipment, a zipper down the middle. On the left side is all my humanness—my selfish thoughts and inclinations, my anger, my resentment, etc. On the

> *I see my heart as having, as part of its standard equipment, a zipper down the middle.*

other side of the zipper is my spiritual side. It is from that side I determine to behave in ways I know to be kind, unselfish, and gracious, as well as to reflect the fruit of the Spirit.

Many times my desire is to respond from the left side; after all, that's the quick and easy way. However, the ramifications can be enormous, and though I have and still do respond from the left side, I'm never pleased with myself when I do. Nor do I like the tidying up that's necessary as a result.

So when Beth asked how I would feel about the resumption of her search, I quickly had to determine from which side of my heart I would respond. Because I love her and want what is best for her, I couldn't possibly respond from the left side. If I did, I would have said something like, "Are you kidding? You talk about rotten timing. The last thing in the world I feel the emotional stamina for right now is agreeing to your finding your birth parents. I've just lost my husband to death and my son to marriage. Now you're telling me I'm going to lose you too! Why do you need to investigate at all? Have you no idea how threatening your request is? Forget it, forget them."

Though I think those feelings were normal, I had no right to put them on Beth. If I had, we would have come to a major crossroads in our relationship. She would have concluded that my needs were more important than hers and that she was responsible for my emotional well-being at the cost of her own. In addition to that, she would have come to resent my feelings. With her mounting resentment, she would probably begin to feel guilty about those emotions she felt for me as well as guilt that she wanted to know her roots at all.

These would be difficult ramifications to tidy up. For Beth's sake, I could not even consider that kind of personal transparency. She has since learned of my emotions during that time, but they were revealed at a more appropriate hour and a less emotional period in my life.

So when Beth made her announcement about beginning her search, I fixed a reassuring smile on my face and told her she could do so with my blessing and full cooperation.

She's Mine!

Now I want you to know that I did not respond to myself or to God with all that trumped-up charitableness. To do so would be to put myself into a state of denial. I admitted to myself and expressed openly to God all the junk surging out from the left side of the zipper.

I always figure I might as well *tell* God about that ugly stuff since He knows what's going on in me anyway. In fact, I find it wonderfully liberating to talk to God with my humanness showing in all its unattractiveness and not have to worry about what is best for Him. God is the strong one and not I. He doesn't need my diplomacy, and neither does He fall off His throne when I tell Him what He already knows about my feelings—even when that feeling is anger.

So with that freedom, I told God I thought His plan was insensitive. I had just lost my husband in May; Jeff had done the normal, preferable, and healthy thing and gone off and married in June; and now here was Beth wanting to find some people who I wished didn't even exist! What if she found them and liked them better than me? What if she felt great kinship and relief and wanted to be with them instead of with me? I also told God He was overestimating my ability to absorb losses. I was no hero, never had been, and knew I never would be. In addition, I warned Him that 1 Corinthians 10:13, which says we won't be asked to bear more than we are able, was in serious jeopardy with me!

I also explained that I really didn't understand His plan in making it so clear to us that Beth was chosen specifically for us when He now seemed to be rearranging the plan. Maybe He was even returning my daughter to the "other mother." I railed on about that for a while until God interrupted me with a thought that jolted me: *Beth is not your child. She is Mine!*

The more I pondered that thought, the quieter I became. I knew it to be true. What followed was a torrent of other realizations. Because Jeff was born of my biological union with Ken did not make Jeff mine, either. In fact, I cannot and should not feel a sense of ownership with my children. They had been entrusted to me for a period of time, but they were not, nor were they ever intended to be, my possessions. They were not created for me; they were created for Him.

I would always be the earthly parent with all the privileges that accompany that position, but I had to remember that He was, is, and always will be the Father. And if the Father willed, for reasons beyond my comfort zone, to have Beth meet her biological parents, that was not for me to decide. It was, however, for me to decide to trust His sovereign design as well as His loving Father's heart.

It took me nearly a week to assimilate and then accommodate these thoughts. And I want to assure you that only God's enabling brought it about; as I said earlier,

I'm no hero. That was a very difficult week, but again, because I love Beth, had committed her to the Father in a formal dedication service when she was an infant, and knew from Whom she was a gift, I had no choice but to release her.

As I write this some six and a half years after the initial struggle, I continue to need to release her in numerous ways, as I do Jeff. Releasing my children to be fully themselves with their own hard-won convictions and preferences is a task I'm committed to and a task that challenges me. Each time I must let them go again requires the Father's enabling.

"I Found Her, Mom"

Some months after I gave Beth my blessing to search for her birth parents, I was in my office having completed a day of counseling and was returning a few phone calls before heading home. I was startled by a knock at my office door and thought, *Marilyn, did you leave someone in the waiting room who has an appointment? That person probably already has abandonment issues; you're certainly not helping!*

The door then opened and there stood our beautiful brown-eyed, auburn-haired Beth with a little piece of paper in her hand. As she walked toward me in what seemed an interminable length of time, I knew that when she reached my desk I would experience a moment that would forever change my life. And indeed it did. As she handed me the paper, she said, "I've found her, Mom.

That's the name of my birth mother, Sherry Boothe. She lives in Naperville, Illinois, and I'm going to call her in the morning."

Sledgehammer.

Zippered heart.

We chatted a while about what Beth felt and she assured me that, yes, she was prepared for a possible rejection. At age twenty-three, she felt strong enough to deal with it should it occur. She promised to call me as soon as she talked to Sherry. (Beth shared an apartment with a girl-friend, so I couldn't even eavesdrop.)

When Beth finally called the next day, her open-ing line was, "Mom,

Each time I must let them go again requires the Father's enabling.

it was incredible! We talked for nearly two hours and—"

I interrupted her enthusiasm with, "No, no, Beth. I want you to start at the very beginning. Start with 'ring, ring, ring.'"

She agreed then to give a more detailed account that went something like this:

"Ring-ring-ring.

"'Hello?'

"'Hello, is this Sherry Boothe?'

"'Yes, it is.'

"'Well, my name is Elizabeth Jean Meberg, but I was christened Patricia Ann Boothe, and I think you are my birth mother.'"

Apparently there was a gasp on the other end of the line, and then Sherry said, "Beth, oh Beth! We have been praying for this moment for twenty-three years! Is this really you? Were you born in Los Angeles on August 16, 1967? Were you adopted through Evangelical Welfare Agency in Whittier, California?"

Beth was right; the conversation was incredible. Sherry and Steve (the birth father) had been high school sweethearts who married three years after Beth was born. They had three more children, two daughters and a son. Steve is a Baptist minister in the Baptist General Conference, a denomination whose president is my cousin Dr. Bob Ricker. Bob and his wife, Dee, had been in our home many times as Beth was growing up, but they had no knowledge, of course, that Beth's biological parents would pastor under Bob's administration. (Does God have style or what?)

Tired of the Secret

As the months went on, Beth talked many times with Sherry and Steve, and so did I. They were lovely, gracious, warm, and deeply committed believers who loved and served God with humble passion. Such dear, sincere people whose ministry God was blessing were impossible not to like. Actually, they became impossible not to love.

I wasn't surprised when Steve called me the first week in January 1991 and said he wanted to know if it was all right with me if he introduced Beth to his congregation. In addition, he wondered if I would be willing to come to that service along with Jeff and Carla.

I felt a protective surge for Steve and his ministry and assured him we would all be there. But what about his congregation? Was it a risk he really wanted to take? What if his sharing this story meant he would have to leave the ministry? What did Bob think?

Steve said Bob had given his consent as long as I was in agreement. And Steve had decided to trust his congregation to extend grace toward him. If they did not, he could always go back to the accounting profession he had left before going to seminary. I asked him why he was willing to take the risk, and I'll never forget his response.

He said he was tired of the secret. (The various twelve-step programs contain a statement that a secret has no power once it has been told.) Many times Steve had longed to talk about his feelings, his experience, and his many questions about what happened to the baby he and Sherry had been advised to forget. Very few people knew about that baby, but most of those who did had told them to put "it" all behind and to move on as if "it" had never happened. But now, God, the heavenly Father, was doing a new work in Steve and Sherry's lives. Steve felt it was time to talk about "it." I again felt that familiar deep silence within myself.

Before talking about that pivotal Sunday, I need to tell you that Beth met Steve and Sherry along with their young adult children, Amy, Laura, and Eric, for the first time in December, a month before we would be introduced to the congregation. That first meeting was very sweet, and as a result, the foundation was laid for Steve and Sherry to want to introduce Beth to their extended family members as well as to the church family.

Beth flew to Chicago for that memorable service a week

before I did. She stayed with the Boothes, awaiting my arrival Friday and then Jeff and Carla's on Saturday. Steve and Sherry met my plane at Midway Airport and drove me to their home in Naperville.

I hardly need to tell you how peculiar that airport meeting was. Here I was, introducing myself to two lovely people, a pastor and his wife. They greeted me warmly, asked if I was hungry, and apologized for the cold weather. They just happened to be the biological parents of my daughter.

The whole time I was eyeballing them sideways and noticed that Beth's beautiful dark brown eyes looked exactly like Sherry's, and their profiles were so similar it gave me whiplash. But I was saying things like, "No, I'm really not hungry," and "The weather doesn't feel as cold as I had expected."

Mercy!

On Sunday morning, Beth, Jeff, Carla, and I were sitting in the back row of the church, feeling a bit anxious and fidgety. I noticed that people kept turning around to stare at us. I guess it was pretty obvious we were visitors. What was also obvious was that so many of the people turning around and looking at us had auburn hair and brown eyes. *Good grief, Beth is probably related to everyone of them in one way or another,* I muttered out of the left side of my heart. What I didn't know then was that Steve had five brothers and Sherry had four brothers, all of whom were there that Sunday with their wives and children. So I actually was accurate in my mutterings; she *was* related to half the congregation!

When Steve began his sermon, a sense of expectancy filled the room. Something unusual was going to happen, but the congregation didn't know what. (They too had probably noticed the unusual preponderance of auburn hair and brown eyes.) Steve introduced his topic of God's grace and spoke movingly of it. He then asked Sherry to join him at the pulpit, and holding her hand, he told the story of how twenty-three years ago they had a baby they had chosen to entrust to God and relinquish to adoption. He took full responsibility for the youthful excesses that resulted in her conception, but with deep emotion spoke of God's grace and willingness to forgive their sin and even call them to full-time Christian service. He then described the phone call Sherry had received several months ago through which God, in His ultimate showering of grace and tangible show of forgiveness, brought the baby-now-young-adult back into their lives.

After a long pause, and in a husky voice, he said he was privileged to introduce this young woman to his family and church congregation. Would she please join them at the platform? I was praying fervently that the congregation would give a positive response, for I knew this wasn't an easy moment for Beth.

As she stood to her feet and began her walk down the aisle, the silence was broken by what at first was a smattering of applause that then built and built until the entire church was swept up with the warm and enthusiastic sound of clapping hands. I tearfully sighed and sat back in appreciation for God's showering of unconditional love.

Enveloped in the warmth of his congregation's approbation, Steve began to describe the loving, Christian home in which Beth had been reared and how he wished her father could be there today. However, by way of introduction via Chuck Swindoll, Steve read the dedication Chuck had written in his book *Rise and Shine* in appreciation for Ken and his years of friendship as well as his competent leadership in the church. Steve then introduced me as well as Jeff and Carla, and we joined everyone on the platform, which now included Amy, Laura, and Eric. The service concluded with all of us singing "Blest Be the Tie That Binds." A reception followed in the church basement, where we met the many other brown-eyed auburns as well as the relatives without the hair-eye dress code. Several hours later, still wrestling with the clamorings of the left side of my heart, I boarded a plane, alone, and headed home.

A Larger Picture of Life . . . and of God

I began the telling of this event by saying the experience was and continues to be one of loss for me as well as one that has enlarged my interior landscape. It is a loss because I now share Beth as a daughter, and that had never been my expectation nor had it been my desire. However, when I say "share a daughter," Beth is eager that I know she will always consider me her mother, and no one could ever change that deep bond. She affirms that sentiment for me with innumerable gestures and expressions of love. So by "sharing" I mean there is and will continue to be a sharing of Beth's life with the Boothes. Sherry helped when Alec was born. That suggestion was mine. For, in spite of the complexities of my feelings, I love Sherry and sincerely wish her a sense of involvement with one whom she too relinquished unwillingly.

In addition to gaining the deep conviction that Beth is not my possession any more than she is the Boothes', I have been privileged to see a much larger picture of life and God than I had before. When we were all singing "Blest Be the Tie" during the church service, I was completely aware God had ordained that very moment in which we all, His children, should join together on that platform. The Father had granted me the pain and joy of relinquishing Beth, who was always His, and to see Him work out in the lives of others His plan for an even sweeter experience of His love, tenderness, and forgiveness.

Pulling Up the Zipper

More often than not, I feel deeply honored to be so used. However, when the left side of my heart becomes noisy and belligerent (as it did on the plane ride home from the church service), I have to sit down and talk to it out of the right side. Unfortunately, sometimes that seems an unending dialogue. But eventually resolution is reached . . . until the next time. As long as I am human, I am going to have a yacky, complaining left-of-the-zipper side. But He takes that side as well as my more spiritually developed side and embraces me, encourages me, listens to me, and never ceases to love me. He is, after all, my Father, whichever side of my zippered heart has the upper hand at that moment. And that thought brings me great joy and a cheerful heart.

There is a temptation for me to write more specifically here about my concept of the zippered heart, how it works and how to make peace with both sides of it. But that subject is complex enough to demand a book of its own.

When the left side of my heart becomes noisy and belligerent . . . I have to sit down and talk to it out of the right side.

However, let me say that our peace as well as our cheer are greatly enhanced as we acknowledge and then accept these warring, opposing sides of our hearts. To deny or ignore the left side of the zipper is like pretending we don't notice ten little shoe-chewing, rug-soiling, furniture-dismantling puppies tearing through the house. They are there; they must be dealt with. Our humanity can get just as out of control as those puppies.

For me to pretend, ignore, or deny that my world did not feel dismantled as a result of the "Boothe entrance" would mean order could never be restored to the zippered left. But acknowledging the dismantlement, seeking the restoration of God's presence, and thus pulling up the zipper to merge the two sides of my heart meant I didn't have to live in the puppy chaos. God entered the chaos and restored order. His entrance was my choice, my decision, and that choice always produces a state of cheer.

4
Can't Get No Satisfaction

He is the Rock, his works are perfect, and all his ways are
just. A faithful God who does no wrong, upright and just is he.

—Deuteronomy 32:4

There I was, in one of my favorite vehicles, a convertible, skimming along the Kauai shoreline, which rightfully boasts of possessing some of the world's most intensely turquoise-colored waters. To my left was a lush profusion of greenery spilling over rocks and ledges.

As the gentle trade winds attempted to disrupt my immovable hair, I thought, *This is one of the most spectacularly beautiful spots on earth. It has all the ingredients to qualify for a perfect place: ideal temperature, blue skies punctuated with cotton-ball clouds, and the most compelling, honey-colored sand I've ever seen. Everything I love has all come together to meet me here in this one spot. This is a perfect place, and I should be having a perfect moment.*

But it didn't feel perfect.

Impatiently, I took inventory of myself. I was aware of a mildly persistent headache that had been hanging on for several days. Plus, I was sporting a bit of a sunburn resulting from my resistance to putting up the top on the convertible. Also, just a few hours ago, I had plunged into a delicious platter of macadamia-nut pancakes slathered in coconut syrup. They seemed to be having some sort of altercation with my digestive system. In addition to these challenges, my left sandal strap kept unhooking when I walked, causing me to lurch off course suddenly and without warning. I hated these innocuous circumstances for combining to rob me of a perfect moment.

Several days later, I stood in front of the magnificent Akaka Falls near Hilo and watched the water tumble into a giant bowl of rock surrounded by brilliantly green plants. I was aware once again of the botanical wonder of Hawaii. That would have been a nearly perfect moment because I no longer had a headache, my sunburn had toned down, and my tea and toast were in perfect harmony with my body. Not only that, but I also had purchased new sandals that didn't toss me into the foliage. But mercy! The humidity was palpable, and of course, the food was expensive—good, but expensive.

When asked how the trip to Hawaii was, I enthusiastically responded, "Absolutely wonderful—for the most part—but you know, nothing's perfect."

The Impossible Quest

Of course we all know nothing is perfect—don't we? Yet why do we continue to feel restless and on a quest for perfection? What makes us think it's attainable? And how can we find cheer when we're muddling about looking for perfection?

After every positive statement, it's so easy to add, "But you know, nothing's perfect." It reminds me of a '60s song the Rolling Stones made popular: "Can't get no satisfaction, . . . I tried and I tried, but. . . ." Well, you get the point.

Flirting with perfection can be far more chronic than simply noticing the "less thans" on a vacation. For example, when Ken and I bought our first house, I was so excited I could hardly contain myself. The house had three bedrooms, two baths, high beamed ceilings, a huge fireplace in the living room, and a fenced backyard with beautiful shrubbery and a well-manicured lawn of dichondra grass.

How can we find cheer when we're muddling about looking for perfection?

Our son, Jeff, was three months old when we moved into this house that was perfect for raising children, drinking tea under the trees, and chatting with neighbors over the fence. We were ecstatic.

A flaw in our perfect house cropped up when we discovered how delicate dichondra can be. It requires one to crawl around each day with tweezers and a magnifying glass to tweak out small weeds which, if left to themselves, will suddenly attack the vulnerable dichondra and suffocate it.

One morning, when we awakened to a malicious weed takeover, Ken dashed out and bought some high-powered weed-killer guaranteed to take care of the weeds' murderous instincts. He sprayed and squirted everything thoroughly. The next morning the only green things left in the backyard were our patio chairs. Nonetheless, we loved this home and even made peace with the sturdy rye grass, which replaced the neurotic dichondra.

However, within a few years after our daughter, Beth, arrived, we found ourselves yearning for a swimming pool and more space. After all, we reasoned, wouldn't it be great for the kids to have a pool and invite their friends over to swim while we lounged around the pool's edges? Besides, we wanted to be closer to our church, and as the kids became involved with various youth activities, it seemed only logical and maybe even spiritual to find a bigger as well as a better-located home. We loved our first house but, well, nothing's perfect.

You cannot imagine the excitement we felt when we moved into our new home, complete with swimming pool. We had huge parties in our huge backyard.

We noticed, however, that often we wanted to go to the beach instead of always being by or in the pool. The beach was nearly an hour away. Wouldn't it be fantastic to live at the beach? Wouldn't it be fantastic to live at our very *favorite* beach, Laguna?

After the kids were grown and gone, Ken and I bought a home in Laguna Beach. We couldn't believe our good fortune.

But, you know, it's amazing how foggy it is at the beach. It will sometimes be shrouded in fog, when only a few miles inland the sky is clear. I find fog a bit depressing, especially if it doesn't burn off until evening. But, as I've said, nothing's perfect.

Surprised by Imperfection

Have you noticed the pattern? We didn't dislike any of our homes; it's just that something was a bit off with each of them. It wasn't that the trip to Hawaii wasn't wonderful; it's just that . . .

I think we were a bit slow to learn that life isn't perfect. We claimed to know that, but we were still surprised to find that not only were our houses imperfect but so also were we and our kids, our friends, and for that matter, our church. Reluctantly, we had to admit everything in life was a trifle off—everything.

What draws from us even more intensity than the search for the perfect vacation or house is our search for the perfect mate. In my years of counseling with couples, frequently I would hear comments like, "I thought we were perfect for each other, but something has changed. Now we seem to be bored; we hardly ever talk anymore." "He was just right for me. I knew he was the one, but then I realized he really had a temper—sometimes he actually scares me." "At first we were all over each other, but neither one of us seems to be interested in physical closeness anymore. I guess we're too tired." "Maybe I never really loved her in the first place. I just don't feel anything."

Although I heard another comment less frequently, it was one that broke my heart: "I hate to hurt my husband, but I'm involved with someone who makes me feel so alive, even tingly. I can't bear the thought of breaking up our home, but I only feel alive in his arms. I can't go back to that feeling of deadness. He's everything I've been look-ing for."

Not only is this family about to face the trauma of dis-ruption, but I also know that if this new couple stays together long enough, they too will realize that each has flaws, and neither is perfect. Then we start the cycle over again. The comments become: "I made a mistake. I truly thought he was perfect for me. I guess I was wrong."

A troublesome myth has been circulating for centuries. That myth would have us believe that somewhere, some-how, someone "out there" is waiting for us. When we finally find each other—well, it will be perfect. Do you remember the heart-wrenching rendition of "The First Time Ever I Saw Your Face" sung by Roberta Flack?

> The first time ever I lay with you
> And felt your heart beat close to mine
> I thought our joy would fill the earth
> And last till the end of time.

Those last two lines speak to the universal hope for a joyful love so monumental, so overwhelming, so encompassing, and so enduring it will last forever. That, unfortunately, is the myth people buy into, and that myth keeps some of us on the quest for the perfect other.

> *A troublesome myth . . . would have us believe that somewhere, some-how, someone "out there" is waiting for us.*

And the myth is perpetuated, not only in music, but also

in books and movies. You may remember the best-selling novel *The Bridges of Madison County,* and the subsequent movie starring Meryl Streep and Clint Eastwood. In it we meet the passionate Italian Francesca Johnson who finds herself with a well-meaning but ploddingly dull husband and her two very ordinary children living on a farm in the middle of Iowa. Robert Kincaid, a photographer for *National Geographic,* is shooting the covered bridges of the area.

Francesca's husband and children have left home for several days to go to the state fair. Francesca and Robert meet in front of her farmhouse as he asks for directions. Shortly afterward, he comes to her home for a glass of iced tea, which evolves into dinner and ultimately into several nights of erotic and perfect love. Robert wants her to leave with him and share his exciting life of travel and photography. Though she admits her life on the farm is not what she had dreamed, she decides not to go. The prospect of leaving with Kincaid is vastly appealing to her, but her commitment to the children and her husband keep her from yielding to her heart's desire.

This plot underscores the message of the myth: If you wait long enough, even if you live on a farm in Iowa, your perfect love could appear and sweep you off your feet right in your very own kitchen! The book's compelling element is not the love story. That plot is ages old. It is, instead, the perpetuating of the myth that two people finally find each other and, as a result, experience perfect love.

Am I saying there's no hope for lasting love? Absolutely not! I'm saying there's no hope for *perfect* love. Because we are imperfect, flawed persons, we can't possibly experience anything but an imperfect and flawed love relationship. In fact, true love is loving in spite of imperfection. True love is accepting each other's flawed states and choosing to build a strong and committed relationship anyway.

Taking Off the Mask

This actually is a major cheer-up thought because the most satisfying love is to be loved in spite of being known. Don't we relax into a state of contentment when we no longer have to wear a mask, the function of which is to imply we are more "precious" than we really are sometimes? We can toss the mask and allow ourselves to be seen even when we are unlovable. When we experience being loved in spite of our unlovableness, we've discovered what love is. When we can return that accepting love, we experience a most compelling reciprocity.

And that, incidentally, is the way Jesus loves us. He knows our history, and He knows the sin in that history. Yet because of the unconditional love He feels for His children, when we confess our sin, He forgives us and receives us without condemnation. And His love is perfect.

> *True love is loving in spite of imperfection.*

Cheer Up!

Now let me again raise the question, why do we keep looking for the perfect whatever in spite of never having experienced it?

We were created for perfection. In fact, we were originally placed in a perfect environment. In Eden there were no lingering headaches, digestive challenges, or unsettling sandals. No house would be too large, too small, or too far from the beach. God would supply our desire for the perfect mate as He brought that perfect other to us. God's original design for each of us was to live in a state of perfection. We were created for that experience, and we were created for that expectation.

So what happened? Simply put, Eve disobeyed God and convinced Adam to disobey as well, and the consequence of their disobedience was they were banished from Eden. That meant they lost the perfect environment, the perfect experiences, and the fulfillment of perfect expectations The reverberating aftermath of their disobedience is our yearning and questing for that which was lost to us. This, then, is why Jesus said, "Here on earth you will have many trials and sorrows" (John 16:33, TLB). It all started with Adam and Eve.

Now, is this so depressing we must dash into the kitchen for a cup of restorative tea? You'll undoubtedly receive momentary comfort from a good (though not perfect) cup of tea. But the loss of perfection need not overwhelm us or depress us. Because Jesus very pragmatically stated we could expect imperfect "stuff" in this world, He prepared us to live a reality-based existence. That knowledge can keep us from being surprised when the trials and sorrows come.

Despite Jesus' warning, often when we experience tribulation we are stunned into a state of self-examination and self-incrimination.

"What did I do wrong?"

"Did I bring this on?"

"Am I being punished?"

"Could this have been avoided?"

"Have I not prayed enough, read Scripture enough, witnessed enough, tithed enough?"

The enemy of our souls would love to see us crawl up on that condemnation treadmill and watch us as, with increasing fatigue, we lose our victory and forget that Romans 8:1 states, "There is now no condemnation for those who are in Christ Jesus." We lose sight of the second half of John 16:33, which states, "But be of good cheer, I have overcome the world" (NKJV). That treadmill not only destroys our victory, our sense of value, and our well-being, but it also destroys our faith.

Jesus didn't say, "You've blown it again. Buck up." Or "get a grip." When He said, "Cheer up," He gave us a reason: "I have overcome the world." His statement gives us cause to be of good cheer and a foundation on which we can rest confidently in the midst of sorrows. Our part is to leap off the treadmill and take God at His Word: "There is now no condemnation." Why? Because I am in Christ Jesus.

Not only can we relax in His provision in the midst of our trials, but hopefully we also can quit the constant, guilt-riddled introspection about our possible responsibility for the pain of life. Then we can focus on being of good cheer and remembering that Christ has overcome all the stuff—big as well as the small—that makes life so imperfect.

Let's repeat: Imperfection, trials, and sorrows all started with disobedience in the Garden. Eve fell for a Satan-devised lie, drew her buck-passing husband into it all, and lost paradise. But we can be of good cheer because Christ has overcome the deficits accrued to our account because of Eden.

Now, of course, some trials and sorrows do come to us as a consequence of our poor choices. And some sorrows are ours because we willfully have chosen to yield to the persistent impulse to sin. But that's a different story and not the focus of this chapter.

My intent in these pages is to remind you that nothing in life is perfect because perfection was lost in Eden. But the flip side of this negative is fully understanding and accepting that life will never be perfect and neither will any experience or relationship. If we can accept that, we can quit looking for it, blaming others or ourselves because we can't find it, and even come to a place of peace about that loss. In fact, we might even cheer up a bit as we quit the search . . . the pressure to find perfection is over. That gives me the energy to settle down to a platter of pasta that is a trifle overdone with a touch too little garlic—and not lose my joy.

5
Foretaste of Things to Come

Blessed assurance, Jesus is mine!

—Fanny J. Crosby

Our daughter, Beth, came tearing into the house one morning with a look on her seven-year-old face that meant *I have an idea too big for the universe!*

"Mama," she began, "we could have a horse! It could play in the backyard, drink from the swimming pool, and sleep in the garage. We have plenty of room. I just decided!" Whenever Beth "just decided" anything, it took a good bit of energy as well as creativity to move her away from her conviction.

She countered each of my arguments against a horse with the same statement, "My teacher says taking care of a pet helps ya learn 'sponsibility." Every now and then Beth would broaden her argument with, "I need to get that 'sponsibility sometime, ya know."

Ultimately, we worked our way down from a horse to a hamster. She reluctantly agreed one could learn 'sponsibility with a small animal just as well as with a large one. That issue settled, Beth and I went to the pet store, where she selected Sugar from a squirming throng of other hamsters. We also bought a Plexiglas cage, an exercise wheel, and special hamster food guaranteed to maintain Sugar's robust health.

Initially, the whole family took an active interest in Sugar, but her utter indifference to us squelched any anticipation we may have had of meaningful relatedness. After all, the whole purpose was to give Beth an opportunity to develop "sponsibility."

Several weeks after Sugar became a family member, Beth announced she was sure Sugar was bored. We all felt slightly bruised. How could she be bored? She had a lovely cage, wheel, food, and all of us at her disposal should she want us.

Beth described a Plexiglas round ball that her friend Suzie had for her hamster. She put the hamster in the ball, snapped it shut, and the hamster simply roamed around the house in this little ball. When the hamster moved, the ball moved.

So, in an effort to relieve the tedium in Sugar's life, Beth and I once again headed for the pet store and purchased a roaming ball. I don't know who was more delighted with that ball, Sugar or me. We would put her in the ball, click it shut, and off she would go in a flash, bumping into furniture and walls, righting herself, and then speeding off in another direction. It was rather like watching a miniature bumper car on the loose.

What particularly gave me a giggle was guests' reactions as Sugar would flash through a room. A first-time visitor who caught a glimpse of this self-propelled, fur-filled ball moving rapidly and haphazardly through the house and then quickly disappearing found the experience a bit unsettling. Ken and I often pretended we hadn't seen it and professed puzzlement as visitors tried to describe their sightings.

As Sugar's enthusiasm for her ball began to wane, we were all concerned she might be slipping back into her former state of boredom. Often we would find her in her ball dozing in a corner, behind the couch, or under a table. She made little effort to explore anymore. We knew, of course, that hamsters are nocturnal creatures and do most of their wild living at night, but, nonetheless, Sugar was exhibiting signs of lassitude. What could we do?

Beth suggested we buy Sugar a "sky restaurant." Suzie had purchased one for her hamster, and it had seemed to raise its flagging spirits considerably. We agreed that might be the answer for Sugar. Later, as I watched her zip up the little cylindrical tube that led to a separate floor, I wondered what would happen to her fragile psyche when she discovered that despite its name, food was never served up there in the sky restaurant's tower.

Predictably, the sky restaurant soon lost its appeal. That made perfect sense to me—the promise of food that never appeared would certainly put me in a slump. With some concern, we realized Sugar occasionally whiled away her time by gnawing on the far-right corner of her cage. It occurred to all of us she might be working on an escape route, but surely she couldn't gnaw through the Plexiglas. Surely the best she could manage would be a dime-size opening.

One night around 2 A.M., I awakened to an odd noise. I poked Ken into startled awareness, and of course, he heard nothing. I lay there as he immediately fell back to sleep and ultimately decided he was right. It was nothing.

Then it sounded again. A hurrying, scurrying sound seemed to come from under the bed. It then trailed quickly to the dressing area and into the adjoining bathroom. I leaped out of bed, grabbed the flashlight, and beamed it into the bathroom. Sugar was staring back at me with her little cheeks and neck stuffed so full of something she was barely recognizable in her lumpiness. Carefully setting her and her cargo back into the cage (The top was off; how had that happened?), I watched with delight as Sugar proceeded to spew forth from her mouth one brightly colored wooden bead after another. The beads would hit the Plexiglas wall and then roll into silence. One, two, three, four, five, six . . . finally, seventeen beads later, little Sugar had disgorged her treasures.

Apparently in her early-morning foray throughout the house, Sugar had discovered the beads under Beth's bed. (Beth and Suzie had been making necklaces to complement their second-grade wardrobes.) I scooped up the beads, thanked Sugar for a wonderful giggle, and went back to bed.

A few weeks later, I returned from work to discover Sugar had escaped again. She had gnawed through the cage corner and was nowhere to be seen. The slider screen to the backyard was slightly ajar, so I assumed she had ventured outside. But my searching was unsuccessful. This time she was gone for good.

When I told Beth about Sugar's escape, instead of the

pained response I had anticipated, Beth was relieved. Her philosophical response was, "That's probably best, Mama. Nothing seemed to make her happy anyway." Noticing my lingering concern, Beth added, "Try not to take it too hard. You did everything you could." Several hours later, she followed me into my study and said, "Would a horse make you feel better?"

An Insatiable Yearning . . .

Oddly enough, Sugar has not receded into the recesses of my memory. She charmed me enormously, but she also seemed to represent the continual searching for something other than what is available. This yearning, or questing, is not the same as the desire for perfect experiences and perfect places. It's far more subtle and elusive. It is, however, sufficiently intense to keep us searching, feeling unsettled, and living on the other side of town from cheer.

Now I can just hear you saying, "Good grief, Marilyn! This is a hamster we're talking about! She just wanted her freedom. You can't make grand life applications from the behavior of a hamster!"

But the reality is I'm not all that different from Sugar. I recognize that ill-defined yearning for something I can't quite give a name to. Sometimes I think I've found that something. But then I realize very soon that wasn't "it" after all. This insatiable quest is part of the trials and sorrows of life, along with things that don't work, having a zippered heart to deal with, and the search for perfection in people, places, and things.

I remember as a tiny child I thought the answer to "it" was simply to be bigger, maybe finally attend school like everyone else in the neighborhood. Or maybe I just needed to be a teenager with more privileges and freedoms, maybe that was "it." I was sure that obtaining my driver's license would be "it." Well, possibly the "it" was going to be realized when I left home and went to college . . . maybe when I got married . . . had children . . . bought a home. Though all these experiences have been gratifying, the sense that something is missing persists.

I recognize that ill-defined yearning for something I can't quite give a name to.

Dorothy Parker captured the elusiveness of our search in her poem, "Temps Perdu."

I never may turn the loop of a road
Where suddenly ahead, the sea is lying
But my heart drags down with an ancient load.
My heart, that a second before was flying.

I never behold the quivering rain
And sweeter than rain than a lover to me
But my heart is wild in my breast with pain;
My heart, that was tapping contentedly.

There's never a rose spreads new at my door
Nor a strange bird crosses the moon at night
But I know I have known its beauty before,
And a terrible sorrow along with the sight.

The look of a laurel tree birthed for May
Or a sycamore bared for a new November
I as old and as sad as my furtherest day
What is it, what is it, I almost remember?

Parker senses that whatever "it" is, she has known it before. But before what . . . before whom . . . before when? She doesn't know, but it quietly, persistently, and poignantly nags at her, an "ancient load" that has its origins in the beginning of time.

The "it" for Solomon of the Old Testament was to return to his knowledge and trust in God. For a time, he chose to ignore God. During that time he was at the top, the wealthiest man in the world but the most miserable. He wrote in Ecclesiastes 2:4–11:

I undertook great projects: I built houses for myself and planted vineyards. I made gardens and parks and planted all kinds of fruit trees in them. I made reservoirs to water groves of flourishing trees. I bought male and female slaves and had other slaves who were born in my house. I also owned more herds and flocks than anyone in Jerusalem before me. I amassed silver and gold for myself, and the treasure of kings and provinces. I acquired men and women singers, and a harem as well—the delights of the heart of man. I became greater by far than anyone in Jerusalem before me. In all this my wisdom stayed with me.

I denied myself nothing my eyes desired;
    I refused my heart no pleasure.

My heart took delight in all my work,
  and this was the reward for all my labor.
Yet when I surveyed all that my hands had done
  and what I had toiled to achieve,
everything was meaningless, a chasing after the wind;
  nothing was gained under the sun.

The tragedy in Solomon's questing was that he knew better. His relationship with God had been meaningful and real. Yet he veered off course, lapsing ultimately into cynicism and hopelessness, much of which is recorded in the Book of Ecclesiastes.

"It's" Not of This World

I can understand Dorothy Parker's ill-defined longing, because she was not a believer. I can understand Solomon's questing, because he strayed from God and what he knew of Him. But for a practicing, believing, sincere child of God like myself, what is the explanation for my "it" quest? Am I simply a malcontent?

Nah, I have too much fun to be a malcontent. So what's wrong with me?

I have just, in the last few years, come to understand my malady, and C. S. Lewis was the person who cleared it up for me. He said:

Most people, if they have really learned to look into their own hearts, would know that they do want, and want very acutely, something that cannot be had in this world.

Creatures are not born with desires unless satisfaction for those desires exists. A baby feels hunger: well, there is such a thing as food. A duckling wants to swim: well, there is such a thing as water. Men feel sexual desire: well, there is such a thing as sex. If I find in myself a desire which no experience in this world can satisfy, the most probable explanation is that I was made for another world. If none of my earthly pleasures satisfy it, that does not prove that the universe is a fraud. Probably earthly pleasures were never meant to satisfy it, but only to arouse it, to suggest the real thing. (*The Best of C. S. Lewis,* Macmillan, 1969)

That means the what's-missing "it" is something I will not satisfy on this earth. It doesn't mean I won't have wonderfully rich, satisfying, and cheer-inducing experiences here. It doesn't mean I won't occasionally fall over in fits of helpless laughter. It doesn't mean I can't luxuriate in the taste of garlic and butter, my favorite flavors. It doesn't mean I can't look into the faces of my grandchildren and nearly burst with pride and pleasure. It simply means I'll find "it" in heaven. And that gives me ample reason to be of cheer.

I love Lewis's sentence that "earthly pleasures were never meant to satisfy it, but only to arouse it, to suggest the real thing." What that thought says to me is that "it" can only get better and better.

For instance, one of my favorite experiences in life is intense and meaningful conversation. I love to really dig in and exchange thoughts with someone on a level of authenticity, vulnerability, and trust. Yet, because of my humanity, I may experience an occasional attention lag. My foot may go to sleep; I might become thirsty or hungry. Or, because it's late, I may lose mental clarity, and my answers no longer stay in sync with my partner's questions.

Even though the conversational exchange was exhilarating, its earthly limitations made it less than perfect. But the time is coming when my foot, thirst, hunger, or fatigue will not be issues. Then I can anticipate hours of unending, perfect conversations. That which I love here is only going to get better there!

The End of the Quest

But I have also had experiences that seemed to me even heaven could not improve on. One of those times occurred just three weeks ago in a bustling, picturesque little village called Blockley, deep within the Cotswolds of England.

Having need of a good, bracing cup of late afternoon tea, I decided also to order something called "sticky toffee pudding." I had never heard of such a concoction, but it was a foretaste of heaven. The brown-sugar, raisin-filled bread pudding swam in an oversized bowl of rich, toffee butter sauce. I will confess to you that I made a bit of a spectacle of myself as I dove into the bowl, slurping, exclaiming, and licking my way through this exquisite taste treat.

When I had resumed my sitting position at the table, I had a deliciously cheerful thought. While I couldn't imagine how to improve on that "heavenly" dessert, eternity would offer a couple of bonus benefits. When I sidle up to a bowl of sticky toffee pudding in heaven, it will not be too rich, and I'll never get too full. But until that day comes, I'm saving my frequent flyer points for another trip to Blockley.

We lost the full satisfaction of the "it" because of the Genesis fall. We seem even to have lost a name for it but can only try to describe "it" in nebulous terms such as "yearning," "longing," and "quest." But "it" is very real and very specific. Once it is satisfied in heaven, we'll all respond with "aha." At last we'll know what it is and how satisfying it is to experience.

For years I felt a trifle guilty that I had an "it" quest. In fact, for years I wouldn't even admit I yearned for "it". I would berate myself for wanting more of whatever and not even know what the "whatever" was. Often in my speaking I quote Saint Augustine, who said, "O God! Thou has made us for Thyself and our souls are restless, searching 'til they find their rest in Thee." I have used this quote as an invitation to come to a place of rest found only in God.

But within myself the niggling voice would say, "Well, why are you still a bit restless, Marilyn? What's wrong with you?" Jesus' statement in Matthew 5:6 also left me with questions. "Blessed are they which do hunger and thirst after righteousness: for they shall be filled" (KJV). Since I've never felt totally filled, I blamed myself. I wasn't doing something right.

But what really put me in a slump was Deuteronomy 4:29: "But if . . . you seek the LORD your God, you will find him if you look for him with all your heart and with all your soul.

I blamed myself for not seeking Him hard enough. Then I'd think, *Maybe we should be in a different church, or maybe I need to pray longer, read Scripture more extensively, or maybe I need a different translation.* More damaging than these thoughts was the idea that *Maybe I'm not good enough, and the "it" is for others but not for me.*

Incidentally, that last thought came directly from the enemy. Anytime we feel diminished or accused of being unworthy, those are Satan's words. Jesus said in Revelation 12:10 that Satan is "the accuser of our brethren" (KJV). We can recognize his creepy voice any-time we feel accused. The Holy Spirit woos us, loves us, and moves us to a place of understanding. He never undermines us, His children, with derogatory messages that make us feel worthless. We are worth the price of Jesus on the cross, which makes us acceptable to a holy God just as we are. (That truth always makes me want to break into a joyful jig!)

Now I know that Saint Augustine, Jesus, and Moses were all acknowledging the restlessness humans would feel in our pursuit of "it." I've learned that I must not quit seeking, that my rest will not be found anywhere but in Him, and that He fills me with His righteousness. I simply must realize that His supply is inex-

> *Anytime we feel diminished or accused of being unworthy, those are Satan's words.*

haustible, and I will never plumb its depths. I can continue to seek, always with the happy knowledge that there is more, and it is not being withheld. That thought is then balanced with the realization that in heaven, finally, all will be told to me, experienced by me, and the "it" will be perfectly satisfied. In the meantime, I can relax, quit feeling guilty, enjoy the satisfactions He brings my way on earth, and recognize the best is yet to come.

Our situation here on earth while we wait is encouragingly expressed in Romans 8:22–24:

> For we know that even the things of nature, like animals and plants, suffer in sickness and death as they await this great event. And even we Christians, although we have the Holy Spirit within us as a foretaste of future glory, also groan to be released from pain and suffering. We, too, wait anxiously for that day, when God will give us our full rights as his children, including the new bodies he has promised us—bodies that will never be sick again and will never die. We are saved by trusting. And trusting means looking forward to getting something we don't yet have. (TLB)

6
Whatsoever Lovely

But the fruit of the Spirit is love, joy, peace, patience,
kindness, goodness, faithfulness, gentleness and self-control.

—Galatians 5:22–23

A cheerfully inclined robber broke into a home late one night with the intention of picking up a few things. Humming softly to himself, he roamed about the living room, periodically dropping items of interest into his black bag and congratulating himself on his skills at breaking and entering.

He was startled from his happy shopping spree by a voice that said, "Jesus is watching you!"

The robber quickly beamed his flashlight in the direction of the voice, only to see a parrot sitting in a cage who once again said, "Jesus is watching you!"

The robber laughed softly. "Oh he is, is he? Since you seem to know so much, what is your name?"

"Nebuchadnezzar," replied the parrot.

The robber laughed again and said, "Who on earth named you Nebuchadnezzar?"

The parrot cocked his head slightly. "The same guy who named the pit bull behind you Jesus."

A Gift of Cheerfulness

We, as believers, know Jesus is no pit bull. He is, however, vigilant and never takes His eyes off us, not because He wants to catch us at something, but because His love for us causes Him to watch out for the well-being of His children. One of the ways He has provided for our well-being is by giving us the capacity to be of good cheer. He has created within each of us a facility, even a giftedness, for being cheerful.

We are not talking about an ability to create humor. Not all people can do that. But all people can develop a cheerful interior. It's an attitude, a way of seeing life, that we can train ourselves to have. For life doesn't always give us a long list of reasons to be cheerful.

I discovered the foundational reason for cheer, knowing Jesus personally, when I was five

He has created within each of us a facility, even a giftedness, for being cheerful.

years old. My conversion was inspired by Leroy Walker's death. Leroy Walker was a turtle who had been tyrannizing Mrs. Boden's vegetable garden. She had no idea where he had come from, and apparently he showed no inclination to leave. In desperation one evening, she walked across the street to our house and asked if I would like to have this turtle for my very own. She insisted on one stipulation: He was not allowed in her garden.

I had not had a pet thus far in my life and was thrilled at the prospect. Getting permission from my parents, I eagerly took on the task of corralling Leroy. I had visions of great, companionable walks, my turtle and I.

Leroy didn't share my vision. In an effort to overcome his reluctance, I managed to tie a string, which was to serve as a makeshift leash, around his neck. The unhappy result was that he merely clunked along the sidewalk, legs and head ensconced in his shell. Our bonding activities were severely limited.

It wasn't long before Leroy began to show signs of the failure-to-thrive syndrome, which concerned me enormously. I knew he longed for his daily romp through Mrs. Boden's garden, but I also knew that my honor prevented me from allowing him to go there. Even though he had free rein in our yard and I provided food the turtle book recommended, he became increasingly lethargic.

One morning I took him out of his big cardboard box for our customary time of fellowship, which consisted of me lying on my stomach and whispering into the caverns of his shell. This time there was no movement. I was horrified. Leroy Walker had died. It wasn't surprising, but it was nonetheless horrifying.

I took my broken heart and Leroy's silent shell into the kitchen, where I fell into my startled mother's arms. My overriding emotion was not grief so much as horror. After all, Leroy and I were not what you would call close; so the loss of the relationship was not what sent me flying into the kitchen. It was the overwhelming realization of what death implied: nothingness . . . no movement. What did all that mean, not just for Leroy but for Marilyn? I had never in my short life contemplated death . . . Why should I? But now, all of a sudden, it was a scary reality.

My mother soon sorted out my major concern, and

talked to me about death. She explained that Jesus died on the cross for the sin that separates me from God. If I acknowledged my sin in confession to Him and received Jesus into my interior being, I need never worry about death. When I died I would be instantly with Jesus in heaven.

Since my dad was a minister, I had heard about the sin thing, but it had not made a lot of sense to me. My mother said sin is the feeling inside of you that wants to do the wrong thing instead of the right thing. Now that made sense! I secretly had wondered if there was a little something wrong with me, because I rather enjoyed doing what I knew I wasn't supposed to do from time to time. It never had occurred to me that such an inclination was a universal malady. So the concept of sin was rather comforting since I wasn't the only one afflicted with it. Even more comforting was the realization that a cure had been found; His name was Jesus.

The Divine Transaction

When I prayed to receive Jesus into my life that morning, I experienced a wonderfully sweet assurance that I had made a meaningful transaction with the God of the universe. I also knew beyond a shadow of a doubt that I could die without wondering about my eternity—just in case I ever was found lying motionless in a cardboard box.

Leroy's death was my first experience with the trials and sorrows Jesus said we could expect on this earth. Now, of course, a turtle's death does not loom large on the screen of life's potential trials and sorrows, but in my five-year-old experience, it was huge.

And it reminds me, as trials in life often do, of Jesus' statement recorded in John 16:33: "Here on earth you

> *A cure had been found; His name was Jesus.*

will have many trials and sorrows; but cheer up, for I have overcome the world" (TLB). What a wonderfully upbeat formula for living. Jesus is saying, in essence, that of course we are going to experience difficulties, and some will be heartbreaking. But we can cheer up in spite of all that. We can maintain our joy in the midst of sorrow. Why? Because He has "overcome the world."

This mind-boggling thought assures me of a way to maintain my balance when life's experiences cause me to teeter. It assures me that my foundational joy does not leave me even though I may not be in touch with it. It assures me that because of Jesus, the Overcomer, I too can be an overcomer in all my trials and sorrows simply because He lives in me. As a result, I have access to His victory and His power over my circumstances.

He says He will never fail me or forsake me (see Heb. 13:5). That means His overcoming power will never forsake me! Why? Because He embodies that power in His person, who in turn lives in *my* person. Now, that makes me want to shed some of my Presbyterian ways and shout hallelujah!

Our cheerfulness rests on our Savior-relatedness. The divine transaction of accepting Christ's death on the cross not only assures us a place in heaven but also a cheerful heart on earth.

That we have access to greater cheerfulness is heartening news. That we may need to change some habit patterns or ways of thinking to more fully experience that cheery outlook can be disheartening for some.

A Habit of Cheerfulness

Let's first make a distinction between a habit and an attitude. The word *habit* is defined as "a constant, often unconscious inclination to perform an act, acquired through its frequent repetition." An *attitude* is defined as "a state of mind or feeling with regard to some matter." It seems to me that, if we first develop the habit of being cheerful, then we in turn will produce the attitude of cheerfulness.

A woman named Genevra will always be an inspiration to me as one who, early in her life, developed a cheer habit. I didn't know the history of this development for quite some time. All I knew was that Genevra was the most fun bank teller in my bank, and because of that I would pass up other tellers just so I could do my banking business with Genevra. We would laugh, talk, and carry on as if no one were waiting in line. The other reason I always waited for Genevra was because of the patience and kindness she extended to me regarding my number phobia.

My math deficit is pitiful. If my salvation were dependent on adding a column of figures and getting the right answers, I would need to take out fire insurance for my future. But Sweet Genevra would add up my bank entries (not even her job) and then good-naturedly make scores of corrections in my transactions. All of this without making me feel like a moron.

After almost a year of enjoying as well as appreciating Genevra, I invited her to lunch so we could giggle and laugh without the pall of incorrect numbers hanging about the environment. She enthusiastically accepted.

As we munched our way through our respective chicken salads (every now and then I use good judgment about my food), I asked her to tell me about her life. A slight cloud came over her face as she told me of her father's alcoholism and her mother's determined optimism to raise three girls as happily as possible in spite of the financial and emotional insecurity the dad's drinking produced.

The cloud faded as Genevra described her mother's fun-loving nature and all the "let's pretend" games they played. Her favorite memory was of a stage platform she, her mother, and her sisters built and the fun they had dramatizing stories for each other.

Genevra told me that at an early age she decided to be like her mother. That meant having fun whenever possible. And when it wasn't possible, Genevra said, "Mother would tell us, 'Just wait long enough, open your eyes, and the fun will be around before too long.'"

The habit of cheerful thinking obviously turned into an attitude about life for both Genevra and her mother. I realized this more fully as I inquired about Genevra's current situation and learned that her only daughter had been killed when she was sixteen years old by a drunk driver as she was coming home from school. Genevra's husband sank into a deep depression shortly after the accident and was still on medication.

More Than a Habit

"Genevra, how on earth do you manage to be so cheerful all the time?" I asked, feeling the enormity of her loss in the pit of my stomach. She studied the table for a minute and then said, "Marilyn, there just is no other way to be. If I can't at least laugh and have some fun, there isn't anything in life but pain. I've known enough pain, but I'll never know enough fun. I choose that every day."

Genevra was not only an inspiration to me, but she also was a puzzle. She had no faith system and professed no interest in developing one. Not long after our lunch together, I spoke at a Christian Women's Club luncheon in our community and invited her to attend. She later told me she had a great time and loved the funny stories I told. She never mentioned her reaction to the gospel that had also been a part of my message.

Several weeks later, during yet another chicken salad break, I asked her what place God had in her life. She smiled cheerfully and said, "None, Marilyn, absolutely none."

My efforts to talk about her views about God were met with a soft pat on my wrist and the door-closing statement, "Give it up, Marilyn. I'm not interested."

I honored her wishes; we continued to laugh and carry on in the bank, and occasionally, we had lunch. That was twenty years ago; I've moved to another community, and I've lost track of her.

Genevra was a puzzle to me because I had trouble fathoming her ability to develop such a genuine cheer attitude without God as the foundation. I have since come to realize that nonbelievers can indeed develop an attitude of cheer. This mental health habit is enormously helpful to all persons and available to everyone regardless of the existence of personal faith. That is a God-given capacity created within all of us.

But the problem for the nonbeliever is that the cheer habit has no depth. For instance, Genevra had no cheer-inducing belief that her daughter is in heaven. She had no cheer-inducing hope that she would one day see her again. There was no place for Genevra to go with her concerns about her husband's anguishing depression because Genevra didn't pray. She had no concept that the day could come when she would no longer need to "kick in" the cheer habit but could, because she was experiencing the cessation of all pain, laugh spontaneously in the presence of her loving Creator.

I still believe our cheerfulness rests on our Savior-relatedness, because there is so much more to cheer than habit. There is available to us all a relationship with the Author of cheer, and to have earthly cheer and spiritual cheer is a double whammy. Genevra could utilize only half of the package. I have wanted to find her and say to her, "Oh dear, dear Genevra, there is more . . . so much more."

For the nonbeliever . . . the cheer habit has no depth.

Because I have prayed diligently for her for many years and because I know the seed was planted, I have not given up hoping that she will one day have the complete cheer package. I also know that Her Creator cares far more about Genevra than even I do. And that, incidentally, is a cheerful thought.

Making a Choice on How to Think

The Bible clearly provides the guidelines for achieving healthy thinking patterns. Paul said in Philippians 4:8, "Whatsoever things are true, whatsoever things are honest, whatsoever things are just, whatsoever things are pure, whatsoever things are lovely, whatsoever things are of good report, if there be any virtue, and if there be any praise, think on these things" (KJV). I believe Paul was encouraging us to make a choice in how we think. Once we make that choice, we won't be victims of unhealthy thought patterns. Paul then delineated what would be good for us to think about.

I've always had a particular affinity for the message of that verse because of the way it became part of my childhood experience. My father pastored small rural churches in the state of Washington, and it was his custom to visit his church members' homes at least once every two weeks. Generally, these people lived on farms scattered around the little town of Amboy. To call on just two families often took an entire afternoon.

I loved going on these pastoral calls with my dad. I liked spending time with my father, and I enjoyed riding around in the old Model T Ford, which, much to my mother's chagrin, he had painted purple and yellow. This old eyesore coughed, hissed, and belched with such noisy enthusiasm it made me giggle. (Dad told me he felt the car's basic usefulness was that its sounds warned his parishioners several miles in advance that "the preacher was coming." They had plenty of time to hide whatever needed to be hidden and pull out whatever needed to be seen.)

One of my favorite pastoral calls was to Mr. and Mrs. Wheeler's farm. Mrs. Wheeler was the most pleasant, jolly, and "laughy" lady I've ever known. She was exceedingly heavy and, not surprisingly, a fabulous cook. Her husband, who was not as tall as she and weighed at least one hundred pounds less, called her his "Baby Dumpling." She called him "Mr. Wheeler." They had been married for more than fifty years but spoke to each other with the tenderness of newlyweds. I loved being around them.

Mrs. Wheeler (I wouldn't dare call her Baby Dumpling, even behind her back) habitually interspersed her conversation with the phrase, "I was just thinking whatsoever lovely . . ." For example, she would respond to our noisy entrance onto their property with, "Well, Pastor, I was just thinking whatsoever lovely, and here you are!" or "I was just thinking whatsoever lovely when I decided to make a peach cobbler," or "I was just thinking whatsoever lovely when Mr. Wheeler surprised me with a kiss on the back of my neck."

These statements always seemed to inspire wonderfully contagious moments of laughter from Mrs. Wheeler. It was impossible not to join in, even when nothing about her comments seemed especially funny to me.

Lurching home from the Wheelers's one afternoon, I asked Dad why Mrs. Wheeler said "whatsoever lovely" about so many things. Dad was thoughtful for a minute and then replied, "Well, Marilyn, Mrs. Wheeler has a habit. She told me one time she could either think sad thoughts or glad thoughts, and she would rather think glad ones, or, as Scripture says, 'lovely' ones."

I was just thinking whatsoever lovely, and here you are!

It wasn't that Mrs. Wheeler couldn't think of any sad thoughts to consider. I learned some years later that the Wheelers's only child had died of rheumatic fever at the age of six. Apparently, they had made a conscious choice about how they would cope with their loss. They chose "glad" over "sad," and they and those around them were the richer as a result of that choice.

We are all capable of increasing our state of cheerfulness. Being of good cheer is an attitude of the mind made possible by God's enabling power within us. As we remember that Christ, our firm foundation, never moves or wavers, we can, then, in partnership with Him, make choices about our habits of mind that produce attitudes of cheer. The specifics of how we do that are the subject of the next few chapters.

For the time being, remember Philippians 4:7: "And the peace of God, which transcends all understanding, will guard your hearts and your minds in Christ Jesus." Remember, Jesus is watching you, guarding your mind, encouraging you to develop the habit of cheerfulness.

7
Ain't It Awful?

So do not worry, saying, "What shall we eat?" or "What shall we drink?" or "What shall we wear? . . . " Your heavenly Father knows that you need them. But seek first his kingdom and his righteousness.

—Matthew 6:31–33

No, Marilyn, you have to drive. Were I to drive and then be stopped by the police for any reason, I would go immediately to jail!"

I stared at my friend Pat Wenger, wondering if she had some sort of private life I knew nothing about. I had never heard her express fear about becoming an inmate before. I considered the possibility she had had a stroke sometime after breakfast. Perhaps that left her a trifle confused about herself and her future.

I ventured a question. "Why do you think you're on the verge of going to jail?"

"Because there's a warrant out for my arrest," she snapped, "and if I'm stopped, the warrant will appear on the patrolman's computer screen!"

Pat and I had been "shrinks" together for some years; her son had dated my daughter; Pat, her husband, Ken, and I had often gone to dinner, played golf, and barbecued as a group. Never would I have wondered if this dear friend could be involved in some nefarious activities that might send her to jail.

Of course, the entire community is shocked when the CIA uncovers enemy secret agents living in one's very own neighborhood. The reason secret agents remain secret is because they appear to be one of us.

I eyeballed Pat uneasily out of the corner of my eye. Somehow, with the many years invested in our friendship, it didn't seem right for me to abandon her . . . at least not until I found out the severity of her crimes. Of course, she might not be willing to talk specifically about them, but it would be only a matter of time before I read about them in the newspaper anyway. I might as well ask.

Using my carefully modulated shrink voice, I asked, "Would you like to talk about what might send you to jail?"

With a ferocity I had never seen before, she said, "I failed to appear for jury duty, and I'm in violation of Section 209, California Code of Civil Procedures."

It took only a few seconds to mentally remove Pat from the FBI's Ten Most Wanted list, but it took a bit longer to grasp the significance of violating the Code of Civil Procedures. When I did, I couldn't help erupting in whoops of raucous laughter that I'm sure were far more offensive than not upholding Section 209.

Mirthlessly, Pat watched me stagger about her garage as I made feeble efforts to contain myself. In exasperation she said, "You obviously have no understanding or empathy for my situation!"

"Do you think by any chance you might be exaggerating the consequences of your crime?" I managed to say between hiccups. (One of the by-products of out-of-control laughter for me is hiccups.)

"No, I am not exaggerating at all!"

"Well, how do you know you would go to jail?"

"My tax man told me!"

That set me off into another fit of laughter as well as even more severe hiccups. Rather than question the extent of her tax man's knowledge of criminal or civil law, I finally managed to get myself under control, and we set out for the Price Club. I drove.

"Awfulizing" Life

This crazy anecdote is a study in unhealthy mind habits that lead to anything but cheer. What about my thinking when Pat announces to me her arrest by the police is imminent? I immediately take note of her agitation, which then leads me to speculate about her possible undercover work as an enemy agent. Would you call that logical, rational thinking? It sounds more like the responses of someone who has watched one too many James Bond movies. The logical mind says the reason for Pat's agitation is far less dramatic than being caught as an enemy infiltrator.

By the same token, Pat is sure she's going to be hauled off to jail because she didn't show up for jury duty. The logical mind says some reasonable action can be taken before Pat has to say good-bye to her family, friends, and three cups of Starbucks coffee in the morning. Not only that, is it logical to assume that the tax man has sufficient knowledge about the Code of Civil Procedures to make definitive statements regarding the punishment for breaking that code?

It's easy for us to react in irrational ways unsupported by knowable facts. If we regularly respond in these extreme ways, we can develop the mind habit of "awfulizing" our experiences and building them up to be far worse than they really are.

The lady who owns the dry cleaners where I take my clothes for rejuvenation is a classic awfulizer. Yesterday I took a new pair of slacks to her and asked if she could replace the zipper. She looked at the pants, which still sported their department-store tags, and threw her hands into the air. "Can you imagine the nerve of a company making a pair of pants with a bad zipper and selling them anyway?" she exploded.

I, of course, had muttered about that very idea to myself. But by the time the awfulizer had finished telling me about a client whose new zipper would not yield to his very urgent need and the biologically unavoidable consequences of that balking zipper, I was eager to make a quick exit.

Then she began to launch into her personal zipper trauma of that very morning. By this time, I was literally sprinting for my car. Oddly enough, one of the reasons I go to this cleaners is to hear what new awfulizing the woman will carry on about. (They also do fabulous work. If they did not, well, it would be just awful!)

The truth is I do a bit of awfulizing too. Sometimes I awfulize health issues. Because my grandmother, father, and husband died of cancer, I occasionally awfulize myself into a terminal state of my own with only a few months to live. I guess when one feels surrounded by cancer, it can seem logical to assume you could be a candidate.

Sometimes I have what I call my "malady," a painful and most unpleasant condition that only occurs if I become too busy; so I assume it's related to stress. It has

> *I occasionally awfulize myself into a terminal state of my own with only a few months to live.*

casually been diagnosed as diverticulosis. (I say "casually" because I won't submit to any testing. Imagining the procedures—and the results—I awfulize myself into a whole new category of illness.) A wonderful little pill, if taken several times a day for a week, clears everything up, and then I can go for a number of years without experiencing my malady again.

My last attack occurred when I was in Carmel during Beth's enforced bed rest to prevent baby Alec's early delivery. I took my magic pills and was helped, but for the first time, my condition didn't completely clear up. Now several months later, I have awfulized myself into imagining a case of fast-growing stomach cancer that threatens to take me off the planet before I ever finish writing this book, let alone see it published.

My friends try to talk me into a thorough checkup, but I have awfulized that scenario to the point I would almost rather succumb to cancer than try to swallow gallons and gallons of barium, which I would undoubtedly throw up before I could then be x-rayed. Then I'd be forced to return to the gallon jugs and tank up again. (I'm basically liquid intolerant. I've reconsidered and decided hell is a place of not only high-heeled shoes, computers, and sewing machines but also of forced liquid consumption. Of course, liquid intolerance will probably lead to kidney stones . . .)

An ABC Attack on Awfulizing

Albert Ellis, president of the Albert Ellis Institute for Rational Emotive Behavior Therapy, has developed a cognitive approach to personal problem-solving that has influenced me enormously over the years. (I still don't want to swallow barium, though!) In my view, he offers an excellent formula that encourages one to attack the illogical thinking that leads to emotional stress. Now, bear with me as we get a bit technical, but perhaps his approach will help you if you want to change some of your mind habits from awfulizing to cheerfulizing.

His formula is called the ABC's of emotional disturbance; here's how it works. When adversities (A's) happen to us, those adversities are soon followed by emotionally upsetting consequences (C's). People usually think these A's cause their C's. Actually, what is more upsetting is not the C's but the beliefs (B's) we have about our adversities.

Changing Awfulizing to Cheerfulizing

Before you groan and head for the teapot, I think the fog will clear as we apply this formula to my resistance to having a thorough checkup. My A (adversity) is the diverticulosis. My C (consequence) is pain and discomfort. My B (belief) is that I probably have stomach cancer. Ellis suggests I need to put my energies into examining how logical my belief system is because it is there in my beliefs and not in the adversity itself, that my greatest emotional stress originates.

You see, I have complicated my situation by not only fearing cancer but also by refusing the means (tests) by which I could learn the true state of my gastrointestinal condition. All of this has occurred in my belief system, which is: I probably have cancer, and I'll never be able to swallow the barium required for the tests.

What I need to do is argue with and hopefully dispute my irrational beliefs and then replace them with

> *I need to take myself into my office and have a little chat.*

realistic as well as biblically based thinking. This will enable me to reduce the emotional and behavioral disturbance. Okay, how do I do that? I need to take myself into my office and have a little chat. I would begin with:

"Marilyn, what's the worst thing that could happen to you in all of this?"

"I could die before Alec is born and before this book is finished."

"Would that really be so awful?"

"Well, actually, no. I'm going to heaven, where there is no barium. Not only that, I wouldn't have to agonize every year over whether I will get a tax audit and then be fined because I have a phobia about numbers and keep lousy records and probably couldn't even find the record in question should the IRS decide it needs to see the receipt for ballpoint pens I bought in 1992. Better yet, I'd be with Jesus and others whom I love."

"That being the case, if the very worst thing happened, death, you've decided it wouldn't really be that bad after all, right?"

"Right."

"So what's the next worst thing?"

"The tests."

"How logical do you think it is that you will have to swallow gallons of some foul liquid?"

"Well, not gallons, but I think it's three or four cups . . . I guess that's not too bad."

"Do you know for sure that it's foul tasting?"

"No."

"Isn't it logical to assume that the barium could be flavored and not foul at all?"

"I suppose."

I also need to address yet another aspect of my belief system: the possibility of having stomach cancer. If my symptoms ultimately are cleared up with those nice little pills, doesn't it make sense that I probably don't have cancer? And doesn't it make sense that, since these "spells" only occur during times of heavy stress, what I really need to concentrate on is diminishing the level of stress?

Probably the reason I still feel niggling discomfort despite having taken my little pills is that my calendar is a bit too busy and will continue to be that way the remainder of this year. But next year will not be so demanding, I hope, and barium will have no place in my thoughts . . . probably.

Power Pills of Scripture

Now that I've attempted to refute my illogical thinking, I need to reinforce my mind with scriptures that (in this specific case) remind me that my loving God is in control of every circumstance in my life, that it is in Him and in His strength that I do what I do. I have scriptural reason to relax. (One does not need any better reason than that!)

Here are a few of my "strengthening" verses that I have personalized, which makes them sound designed for me— because they are.

The LORD is Marilyn's strength and her song. (Exod. 15:2)

O my Strength, I sing praise to you;
you, O God, are Marilyn's fortress, her loving God.
(Ps. 59:17)

Your strength, Marilyn, will equal your days. (Deut. 33:25b)

As for God, his way is perfect;
the word of the LORD is flawless.
He is a shield
for Marilyn when she takes refuge in him.
For who is God besides the LORD?

And who is the Rock except our God?
It is God who arms Marilyn with strength
   and makes her way perfect.
He makes Marilyn's feet like the feet of a deer;
   he enables her to stand on the heights. (2 Sam. 22:31–34)

The next thing I need to do is memorize these verses and use them as ammunition when my thinking becomes twisted, illogical, and cheerless. I can shoot those negative thoughts full of Bible bullets the minute they show up and keep on shooting until I see a white flag waving. The next step is to settle down to a cup of victory tea and a Scottish shortbread.

I know, however, more battles await me; so I need to keep my ammunition up to date and my teapot hot. That's not illogical, now is it? In fact, it's a sequence of behaviors that are cheer-producing: my personalized Bible bullets, Scottish shortbread, and tea. I like that!

I know more battles await me; so I need to keep my ammunition up to date and my teapot hot.

Now, with my mind habits entrusted to Him who has said, "Let this mind be in you which was also in Christ Jesus," I can again recognize my partnering with Him. If I choose not to uphold my part in the partnership, my thinking can veer off course. In no time I'm sitting on a tall stool beside my dry-cleaning lady energetically awfulizing the perils of faulty zippers.

Taking Our Medicine

Before we move on to other ways to develop an attitude of good cheer, let's recap what we've said so far. Laughter is medicine our Good Physician has indicated we should take when we encounter life's trials and sorrows. Some of those trials and sorrows include death, things that don't work, the temptation to live out of the left side of our zippered hearts, our dissatisfying search for perfection, and our insatiable yearning for something we can't even name.

The first place to look for a reason to be of cheer is to Jesus, who serves as a solid foundation for an attitude of cheer. Christ encourages us to think on whatsoever is lovely in life, a mental habit that can turn into an attitude as we regularly employ it. To avoid awfulizing life, which is pretty awful without any help from us anyway, we need to examine our belief systems for irrationality. Once we recognize that failure to show up for jury duty will probably not result in wearing an orange jumpsuit and working on a chain gang, our adversities and their consequences can be greeted with a great deal more cheer.

8
I Shall Rise . . . I Shall Rise

When times are good, be happy; but when times are bad,
consider: God has made the one as well as the other.

—Ecclesiastes 7:14

My father, Jasper Ricker, was an upbeat man. He grew up as one of ten children in a family that knew nothing but poverty. Born in Moncton, New Brunswick, Canada, he was raised on a remote little farm near Turtle Creek, some miles from Moncton. His family struggled for enough food to eat and clothes to wear. During the harsh winter months, the children took turns wearing the few pairs of shoes they had. That meant they rarely got to go to school except on the occasions when one of them drew the lucky straw.

Dad left home at the age of fourteen to supplement the family income by working in a sawmill. He also determined to put aside a little money for himself so he could move to the United States. Because of the educational deprivation of his childhood, he could barely read or write, but he decided one day he would acquire those skills and receive a college education. Given his circumstances, few people believed his desire was anything but a pipe dream. But Dad saw it all as an achievable goal.

Contrary to expectation, Dad made enough money to relocate to Boston. There, by working three, sometimes four jobs, he saved a sufficient sum to enroll at a prep school. Soon after he started at the school, when he'd barely had enough time to luxuriate in the fulfilling of his dream, the bank in which he had deposited all his cash went bankrupt, leaving him with nothing. Because the bank was not federally insured, he had no hope of recouping his losses. Once again he worked a number of jobs so he could return to prep school. Though devastated and disappointed, he never once thought of giving up.

During that period, Dad's brother Sanford also moved to Boston, where he was exposed to the gospel of Jesus Christ and became a Christian. He shared his faith repeatedly with my resisting father, who felt he didn't need Sanford's Jesus. Dad was not open to any experience he thought might interfere with his personal goals; besides, he wanted to run his own life. In my father's view, God hadn't done such a great job with his Bible-believing parents and their brood of children.

The Holy Spirit, as well as Sanford, worked on my father's resistance for many months until he recognized his spiritual need and invited God to come into his life. God, in His sovereign creativity, then called my basically illiterate father to the ministry. This seemed an unrealistic call since Dad needed money to get back to prep school as well as for the basics. Now, he added going to seminary to his list of things to accomplish.

With unwavering determination and optimism, Dad

partnered with God to complete prep school and ultimately to graduate from Nyack College and Seminary. He also married my mother, and together they served the Lord as ministers of the gospel for more than forty years.

Choosing to Think the Best

I saw my father optimistically and cheerfully face life every day. His optimism was not the tight-jawed, grim, I'll-do-it-or-die variety but was lighthearted in spite of challenges that must have appeared overwhelming.

Was he just one of those fortunate persons who happened to be born with an upbeat point of view? Although I don't discount our inherent temperaments, leanings, and bents, I do not believe we are born as optimists or pessimists. Those are states of mind we choose to develop.

> *I do not believe we are born as optimists or pessimists. Those are states of mind we choose to develop.*

They are learned. We don't learn something without first choosing it, even if that choice is unconsciously made based on our formative environments as children. We choose to think positively, or we choose to think negatively. That choice becomes a habit, which then settles into an attitude.

One of my favorite stories of Dad's childhood was when he sat on the banks of Turtle Creek and told the fish, which refused to bite, that he would rise. Dad told me he would pound his fist on the ground and say over and over again, "I shall rise . . . I shall rise!"

I never understood what the "I shall rise" phrase meant. Each time I asked Dad, he would give me a slightly different answer. For example, once he told me it meant he would rise to the level of educational preparedness for which he so desperately longed. Another time he told me it meant he would rise above the level of grinding poverty in which he and his family lived. As an adult, I now know it meant all of that and more. He was talking about an attitude of not giving in or giving up.

Once I asked him if he ever doubted that he would rise. He told me that after a chat with his Uncle Early in a hayfield one hot, summer day, he never doubted again. Uncle Early had responded to Dad's youthful dissatisfactions with the short phrase, "Think the best and then get it."

Uncle Early, at the age of seventy, had married a pretty woman who was thirty years younger than he, and to all appearances, she adored her elderly husband. Apparently, Dad saw some tangible evidence that Uncle Early's philosophy must work. How else did he manage to marry such a pretty and very young woman? Uncle Seamore, Uncle Early's brother, always told Dad to "never let life get in your way."

These rough-hewn uncles had a profound influence on Dad's thinking as a kid. He simply refused to be deterred from his goal; instead of thinking negatively, he chose to think positively and truly did not let life get in his way.

Training Ourselves to Think Positively

Not only does positive thinking facilitate the achieving of our goals, it contributes enormously to our physical health and well-being. Persons who have a positive frame of mind live longer and are less prone to illness. Scientists believe pessimism causes more stress to the body than optimism. When the body responds to the mind's negativity, it releases an array of *Never let life get in your way.* hormones that provide quick energy. But there's also a down side to this automatic energy supply. Two of these hormones—adrenaline and cortisol—are also potent inhibitors of the immune system. So when we are stressed, parts of our immune system shut down, and the result can be illness.

The movie actor Woody Allen scripts his characters as those who agonize over an assortment of insecurities. They routinely awfulize nearly everything in their lives. In the movie *Manhattan,* Allen plays one of his typically neurotic characters. When Diane Keaton, who plays his girlfriend, announces she is leaving Allen for his best friend, Allen appears to be nonchalant and undisturbed. Keaton demands to know why he doesn't react, and with a heavy sigh he says, "I can't express anger; I grow a tumor instead."

When we train ourselves to think positively instead of negatively, our tolerance for pain is higher, our recovery from illness or surgery is quicker, and even our blood pressure is lower; it might even help those neurotic Allen characters to avoid tumors!

Cheerfulness . . . Tempered by Realism

Having said all this about the value of establishing an

attitude of cheer, let me swerve onto a brief detour (I hope I don't give you whiplash!) and say that some people are so positive they set the gold crowns on the left side of my mouth to jangling. These persons are so mindlessly positive they're annoying. I want to sidle up to their ears and whisper, "Phony!"

One of my most memorable experiences with this kind of shallowness occurred years ago, when our children were very young, and I taught several weekly Bible studies. I loved that period in my life and remember the fun of watching nonbelievers and believers deepen their understanding of who Jesus is and what He promises us as our inheritance when we become the children of God, literally becoming members of His family.

I initially felt especially drawn to a woman in one of these Bible studies. She was pleasant and laughed easily. As the weeks went on, I was aware that this woman's expression never changed. She smiled continuously as I taught, smiled continuously when she was speaking or being spoken to, and even smiled while she sipped her coffee. (I often wondered how she avoided dribbling.) Ultimately, she began to get on my nerves, especially when even our study of the crucifixion produced the same smiling cheerfulness.

Convicted by my growing animosity toward her and suspecting her cheerfulness wasn't real, I made efforts to get to know her better. I learned she had become a Christian as a child, had always been active in church, and had three children and a Christian husband. That all sounded good . . . perhaps she *was* real . . . but she sure got on my nerves! Convicted again by my uncharitable thoughts, I continued to try to learn what made her tick. One day I experienced a breakthrough.

During our sharing time, she smilingly asked for prayer concerning a decision her husband was making about whether he should quit his job, sell the house, and use the equity to support the family so he could devote more time to his personal Bible study and to be more active in their church.

We all sat in stunned silence for a moment. Finally, one of the class members asked her if this plan felt a bit threatening to her. Did she worry about the financial well-being of the family? Was this just his plan or had he discussed it with her before making the decision? What would happen when the house equity was gone?

With an undiminished smile, she said she had learned long ago not to worry about things in life. Then she quoted Matthew 6:31–34: "So do not worry, saying, 'What shall we eat? Or what shall we drink? Or what shall we wear?' For the pagans run after all these things and your heavenly Father knows that you need them. But seek first his kingdom and his righteousness and all those things will be given to you as well. Therefore do not worry about tomorrow, for tomorrow will worry about itself."

Her ability to spontaneously quote the entire passage was impressive, and certainly Jesus was saying in the verses we are not to worry. But she put the capper on the whole discussion by adding that she had the gift of faith and cheerfully quoting Romans 8:28, too: "all things work together for good." She was simply trusting God for her family's needs.

What was so troubling about this woman was not just her relentless smiling but that everything she said and quoted was true—on one level. The problem was her application of Scripture. The truth was, her thinking was wrong. In fact, she was out of touch with reality.

The reality was her husband, as leader of their home, needed to safeguard his God-given responsibilities. He needed to provide for and to protect his family. In addition to that, God had set up marriage as a partnership in which each spouse gives to the other with mutuality, as Christ does to us. This woman was not partnering with her husband. Instead, in the guise of faith, she had become a nonpartici-pant, leaving this crucial decision up to her husband with no input from her. To quote Matthew 6 as a rationale for not working to provide food and drink and saying that God does not want us to worry about those little things was tak-ing that verse out of context. This was not faith, nor was it optimistic thinking; it was a denial of reality.

The woman's thinking reminds me of Mr. Micawber in the Charles Dickens novel *David Copperfield*. Mr. Micawber was a charming, well-intentioned buffoon of a man who lived his life in lighthearted ideal-ism and denial. He, like Dickens's own father, was con-

> *This was not faith, nor was it optimistic thinking; it was a denial of reality.*

stantly in debt and thrown repeatedly into debtors' prison. With each release from prison, he would cheerfully throw a little party, serve his favorite celebratory punch, and assure everyone that sooner or later "something would turn up." In the meantime, his wife and many children nearly starved to death.

We need a dose of realism with our cheerfulness, or we are in danger of living in La-La Land, a world characterized by avoidance and denial.

Reality-Based Faith

It troubles me that denial is often passed off as faith; the two states have nothing in common. If my father, after his conversion and subsequent call to the ministry, had not realistically sought work to replace his lost earnings, he would never have returned to prep school. He had faith to believe God had called him, and he had faith to believe in God's partnering with him through the many challenges that lay before him. He had faith in the God who promises to supply all our needs (like a job—or many jobs). But if my father had sat by waiting for money to come miraculously in the mail or for a diploma to be handed to him because of his great attitude, he would have been living in denial of reality.

Faith enables us to accept the truth and then to search for the means by which we can work out God-assisted solutions. Denial avoids the truth, and as a result, experiences no solution. Faith leads us to solution; denial leads us away from solution. When we're in denial, there's no need for God, and there's no victory from God. Instead, we sit in a haze, smiling vacantly and waiting for something to turn up.

Reality-based, positive thinking is a mental habit well

worth establishing as an attitude. It produces victory in our daily living, it provides health for our bodies, and it provides cheer for our souls.

Our ability to think positively instead of negatively is first a choice. Proverbs 23:7 states, "For as he thinks in his heart, so is he" (NKJV). Our minds determine who we are, how we behave, and how we feel.

> *Reality-based, positive thinking is a mental habit well worth establishing as an attitude.*

The exciting news about all this is that thoughts come before feelings and before actions. That means we have a lot of control over what we do once we learn to think in godly and positive ways. If we are miserable and unhappy, lacking cheer and lightheartedness, it is possible to change those feelings with healthier thinking.

A Formula for Laughter

I don't usually respond to formulas for this and that; they feel a bit too tidy. But I have developed one for cheerful thinking I'd like to toss your way for your consideration. To begin with, I love to laugh. I believe a giggle is always loitering about even in the most devastating of circumstances. I make a point of shuffling through the rubble in search of that giggle.

This isn't denial. I need to feel and express my pain. But I also need to find the light side—and there is *always* a light side! I've noticed that when I laugh about some minor part of a problem or controversy or worry the whole situation suddenly seems much less negative to me. After a good laugh, I can then rethink my circumstances. As a result, that which was threatening may now seem less threatening.

Paradoxically, after I've found the giggle, I am more ready to get serious (it's a more balanced seriousness) and consider the degree and the extent of my negative thinking. I pull those negative thoughts up on the screen of my mind and scroll down through the list, considering each one. (Good grief, I just used a computer image!) The value of this is that it's easier to do battle with what I can see; therefore it helps to "look" at these thoughts to determine how logical they are. After applying the ABC's of the last chapter to them. I now need to determine how I can change those thoughts to realistic optimism. This is when negative thoughts have to be deleted and replaced with those that are realistically positive.

Laughter in the Midst of Sorrow

Let's apply these steps for positive thinking to my father's situation discussed earlier in the chapter. I have no idea what Dad might have laughed about as a relief for his tension when he learned the bank that held his money had folded. But knowing the comical lens through which he viewed life, I would be surprised if something didn't strike him as funny in the midst of that enormous disappointment. Let's say he received notification of his loss on April Fool's Day. There's a thought to chuckle over. Or it arrived on his birthday, and he laughed and told himself this was a present to make any birthday memorable. The reason to giggle doesn't need to be enormous; any angle that provides a lighthearted look at a disheartening situation sets the stage for a positive mind-set.

Second, let's assume these negative thoughts flashed on the screen of his mind (which in Dad's generation might have looked more like a drive-in movie screen or even a window screen than a computer screen!):

1. It will take too much time to start over again . . . I might as well forget graduating.

2. This is too hard. Why not be content with less? Lots of people don't read or write well. I might as well join them.

3. Why not go back to Canada and be a farmer? That's all I'll ever be good at anyway.

4. Everything is working against me. I am basically a guy with rotten luck.

Each of these negative thoughts needs to be seen as a lie or certainly not the whole truth. Now for the last and hardest step: Re-examining each of these thoughts from a positive perspective. Let's tackle them in sequence. He could say:

1. What difference does it make how much time it takes to earn more money? I'm young. I have plenty of time. There are no deadlines on meeting my goals.

2. Of course it's hard, but it's not too hard. I don't want to be content with less, so forget it. Don't mention it again!

3. I don't want to go back to Canada to be a farmer. I'm sick of farming—that's why I left! I'm not going back, so forget that too!

4. I've had a major setback, that's true, but not because something called "bad luck" has decided to run me out of town. I don't believe in luck. I believe in hard work and commitment to my goal. Nothing will shake that out of my head!

Now because Dad was not a Christian at that point, he did not have the much-needed dimension of faith to call on to add clout to his battle against negativism. That came later. However, if he had been a Christian then, each of his refuting points could have included the constant repetition of Philippians 4:13, "I can do everything through him who gives me strength," and 1 Thessalonians 5:24, "The one who calls you is faithful and he will do it."

Renewing Our Minds, Changing Our Attitudes

We, as believers in Christ, can do everything God calls us to do. I am convinced we are all called to replace negative thinking with positive thinking and attitudes. Paul encourages that very thing in Romans 12:2, "Do not be conformed to this world, but be transformed by the renewing of your mind, that you may prove what is that good and acceptable and perfect will of God" (NKJV).

A transformed and renewed mind enables us to manifest an attitude of good cheer. Believe it, think it, and go for it! Don't let life get in your way.

So we add turning negative thoughts into positive ones

to our list of ways to be cheerful, which already includes looking to Jesus, thinking on whatsoever is lovely, and examining our belief systems for lies and exaggerations that lead to irrationality. Next we'll examine how our memories can be a source of cheer.

9
Scrolls of Remembrance

*I remember the days of long ago; I meditate on all your works
and consider what your hands have done.*

—Psalm 143:5

I have always been drawn to people who are quirky or, as
my father would say, "a couple of bubbles off plumb."
Quirkiness draws me like a chocoholic to fudge. That's one
of the reasons I'm loving my association with the other
speakers on the "Women of Faith—Joyful Journey" tour.
We are all a bit off center and enjoy each other tremendously whether we're on stage or off. Because we are so
closely bonded in genuine appreciation of each other's gifts
as well as nuttiness, we've become increasingly less inhibited about showing that on stage.

For example, at a recent conference in Ann Arbor,
Michigan, we encouraged Barbara Johnson to remain in
the Green Room during the afternoon presentations rather
than join us on stage. She had already spoken and was
unusually fatigued that trip. Reluctantly, she agreed since
she could watch everything on the monitors and therefore
wouldn't risk missing our brilliance.

It never occurred to any of us that the stage seating

would be thrown off by Barbara's absence. The staging people had our seats "petaled" around the circular stage in clumps of two, which left Sheila Walsh sitting by herself and no one with whom to clump. As the energetic young women in the Integrity music group moved around the stage leading the fifteen thousand women in the audience in the opening songs, Patsy and I motioned for Sheila to move her chair over to our clump. We had not realized how heavy the chairs were, and by the time Sheila had managed to drag it barely to the center of the stage, she gave up and simply sat down as if she belonged there.

Patsy and I leaped up and lugged Patsy's chair over to Sheila's, placing it directly in front of Sheila, where Patsy deposited herself with majestic aplomb. I grabbed another chair, risking a massive hernia, placed the chair behind Sheila, and sat down as well. The result made us look utterly moronic . . . three women lined up in single file as if we were riding the bus home and no one had told us we had missed our stop.

I looked over my shoulder to see what had become of Luci Swindoll and Thelma Wells and to ascertain why they hadn't boarded the bus. They were so busy with the group singing, clapping, stomping, swaying, and giving each other high-five signs, they hadn't even noticed us.

Our center-stage configuration presented no small challenge to the talented Integrity musicians, whose energetic movements were curtailed by the speaker-jam Patsy, Sheila, and I had created. Later, Barbara told us we obviously were not to be trusted to go on stage without her again.

Zany Memories, Enduring Laughter

I am convinced that one of life's most easily accessible sources of cheer is to remember some of the off-the-wall, crazy things that happen to us. Like our new chair configuration, it doesn't have to be a Big Moment, just something zany and fun. Sometimes those memories are bittersweet as we recall an out-of-the-ordinary moment with a loved one who is now gone. But those times nevertheless provide cheer because that was the emotion felt when the experience occurred. That original cheerful feeling will always remain attached to that memory.

For example, when Ken and I were students at Seattle Pacific University, we put together a ridiculous routine in which we played the roles of spiritual workers on furlough. With disheveled hair, mismatching pants and suit jacket, Ken would stroll on stage and, in a heavy Norwegian accent, begin to make his pitch for money to support our work. The project in need of support was always something pitifully unworthy and without appeal. He would then introduce his unattractive and socially inept wife (me), whose name was Maude Amy. He, incidentally, was named Elias Gulah.

Ken would take his seat at the piano and play our song in one key with his left hand, and with his right, play in another key. Both of us, with heads thrown back, would bellow out a painfully

> *That original cheerful feeling will always remain attached to that memory.*

off-pitch rendition of "Precious Memories." That was followed by Times of Reflection during which I would preach from some Mother Goose rhyme, making exaggerated and grandiose applications to the listeners' lives.

The inspiration from these reflections was heightened by occasional references to the "original languages." These sermons were nearly unendurable for the listener, not only because of the ludicrous applications that were made, but also because I used a voice of one suffering from severe sinus congestion, which caused me to snort, sniff, and cough throughout my exegesis of Mother Goose. People in the audience were constantly blowing their noses in an effort to clear me up.

This Maude Amy–Elias Gulah routine stayed with us after college, and oddly enough, we were asked to do it frequently for groups through the years. One of the most gratifying of those times was when Chuck Swindoll first came to California as our new pastor in Fullerton. Ken and I were asked to do our routine at a huge welcoming party for Chuck and Cynthia. Feeling a bit inhibited, we agreed but figured we would probably have to change churches when it was all over.

Ken began the evening entertainment with his usual disheveled attire and heavy Norwegian accent. When he launched into his impassioned plea for support of our work, Chuck laughed so hard Ken felt inspired to hand out pledge cards. When I began Time for Reflection with my mucous-filled voice and absurd interpretations of "The Old Woman in the Shoe," both Chuck and Cynthia were guffawing and slapping their knees with such enthusiasm we were encouraged to think maybe they liked us and were actually having fun.

When Ken died, he took Elias Gulah with him. Maude Amy is still around, and she has occasionally done solo "Mother Goose preaching" in that same sinus-congested voice. But it isn't the same without Elias. What *is* the same though is the fun of remembering how it was, how people laughed, and how they blew their noses during and after our "services." These quirky memories never fail to give me a giggle.

Remembering the Source of Our Cheer

Now, if all of this sounds like preparation for successful retirement at the "home," where you sit on the porch rocking, picking your teeth, smiling vacantly as you accept your afternoon tapioca, and reminiscing, I want to say that just isn't the case. Pleasant memories can give us an immediate cheer-producing mind switch. We don't have to wait until we're seventy to do it! Those memories can be as recent as this morning or as distant as thirty years ago. All that matters is that the quirky memory cheers you.

Incidentally, the whole "remembering" thing is a biblical concept. God was continually urging His people to remember what He had done for them as a means of encouragement. He wanted them to remember "that God was their Rock, that God Most High was their Redeemer" (Ps. 78:35). I love the image in Malachi 3:16, "A scroll of remembrance was written in his presence concerning those who feared the LORD and honored his name."

Can't you just picture that scroll of remembrance? I see it as being miles long with tight, black-ink writing all over it. Maybe a huge magnifying glass is nearby for reading the fine-print remembrances. The very thought gives me an unexpected perk!

For us believers, remembering starts out by recalling God is the source of our cheer. From that foundational position, we can move into the human realm and remember those experiences that were cheer producing.

A Wonderful Balance of Humor . . . and Love

I was raised in a home with quirkiness in abundance and seriousness in moderation. My mother's background was the opposite of my father's in that her parents and the majority of her ancestors were highly educated and professional. In keeping with the family tradition, Elizabeth Downey graduated from college Phi Beta Kappa and went on to do graduate work.

Though her atheistic inclinations were fairly well established, she was stunned into considering the claims of Jesus Christ through the witness of her Aunt Mary, with whom she stayed during her year of graduate study. Aunt Mary ultimately led Mother into a very sweet and meaningful conversion experience, which produced a tremendous hunger to know the Bible.

Mother had always dismissed the Bible as nothing more than a book of myths, aphorisms, and hyperbolic stories impossible to take seriously. Now that she had a new view, she decided the best way to know the Bible was to go somewhere to study it; so she headed for New York, where she enrolled in Nyack Seminary.

When my mother met my father at Nyack Seminary, it was almost love at first sight. Mom was shy and reserved. Dad was gregarious and outrageous. She was drawn to his fun-loving nature as well as his sincere faith. He was taken with her pretty face and impressive mind. They spent hours talking about God, literature, classical music, and art. Dad was like a sponge, as he listened eagerly to all she knew and all he had longed to know since childhood. He couldn't imagine that this statuesque woman would ever consider marrying a farm boy without family pedigree, prestige, or money. He could offer her no more than sharing his burning passion to preach the gospel wherever God led him. They were married immediately after graduation.

During my growing up years, almost every evening was spent with the sound of my mother's well-modulated voice reading aloud to my father. Together they read nearly all the classics of literature. The memory of her sitting at the end of the couch next to the lamp while Dad languidly stretched out with his head in her lap fills me with soft peace. Dad's favorite author was Charles Dickens. I'm sure it was the writer's high-spirited humor and genius for caricature that so charmed my father.

A character in *David Copperfield* named Mrs. Gummidge for some reason tickled my father enormously. She was a cheerless, dreary person who was constantly saying, "I'm a poor, lone creature, and everything goes contrary with me." Dad taught me to repeat that line when I was four years old. We could be anywhere, and out of the blue Dad would say, "Now, Marilyn, what is it Mrs. Gummidge says?" In the flat voice Dad had coached me to use for this quote, I would assume a grim face and sorrowfully intone, "I'm a poor, lone creature, and everything goes contrary with me."

Dad usually asked me to say the line when we were around people, and the laughing response from them was immensely satisfying to the budding ham within me. The more they laughed the more "lone" I appeared.

My sensitive mother was concerned I might feel exploited in some way as Dad encouraged my Dickens performances. I heard her expressing this concern one afternoon to my father. His immediate response was to promise that, if in any way she felt uncomfortable or feared that I might dislike my role, he would never ask me to do Mrs. Gummidge again. I was tremendously disappointed to have my career in oral interpretation cut short but, at the age of four, didn't quite know how to say so.

Years later, as a student in my mother's Spanish class at BattleGround High School, I was busily talking to a cute boy across the aisle from me and didn't hear my mother's request that I conjugate the verb "be." When I realized what I'd been asked to do and didn't have the foggiest notion how, I assumed a grim face and sorrowfully intoned, "I'm a poor, lone creature, and everything goes contrary with me."

The corners of Mom's mouth began to work in that special way of hers that always culminated in helpless laughter. Ultimately, the entire class was laughing, but I don't think they knew why except that it was fun to see Mrs. Ricker totally lose it.

Mom's gentle seriousness, coupled with her genuine appreciation of Dad's and my unpredictable humor, was a wonderful balance for me as I grew up. I realized not everyone is inherently quirky and not everyone sees the funny side of life first. But I also learned that everyone has the capacity to develop an appreciation for the quirky. I saw it every time Mom's mouth began to work in that special way of hers.

One of my favorite memories occurred in a Chicago airport—a quirky bit of cheer that I'm not sure my mother would approve of my telling publicly. Actually, I'm certain she would suggest to me the story is a bit unrefined. I hope not to offend your sensibilities, but I simply have to risk telling you anyway.

You will remember my writing in an earlier chapter about my first meeting with my daughter Beth's birth parents, Steve and Sherry Boothe. As we were making my travel arrangements to be with them when Steve introduced Beth to his congregation in Illinois, he asked if I could fly into Midway Airport instead of O'Hare. Of course I agreed, but I'd never heard of Midway; so Steve gave me very specific instructions on *Everyone has the capacity to develop an appreciation for the quirky.* cific instructions on where to wait for them since he and Sherry would be delayed about twenty minutes after my scheduled arrival. That was perfectly fine with me. I'm an incurable people-watcher and would have no trouble entertaining myself for a twenty-minute wait.

On arriving, I settled in on the prearranged bench Steve had suggested for my wait. Adjacent to my bench was another one occupied by an elderly man and woman slurping ice cream cones. In a very short time, I formed a tremendous dislike for them. The dislike had nothing to do with the smacking noises they made with their ice cream. It didn't even have to do with the maddening way a small trickle of ice cream dribbled down the woman's chin and then her neck. It wasn't even the distraction of wondering if the trickle would go inside her collar or outside, or why on earth she didn't feel the trickle and do something about it!

What established and then fed my dislike for them was the continual criticizing and demeaning comments they made about the people walking by our benches. They made fun of people's clothes, how they walked, their hair, their noses, and even the expressions on their faces. I looked over at these two, mean-spirited, ice cream-slurping, chocolate-dribbling persons and thought, *Well, neither of you is a prize! You're a couple of negative malcontents who deserve to choke on your slurpings.*

I was soon distracted from these uncharitable thoughts with the realization that I had been sitting there for thirty minutes. Steve said they would be only twenty minutes late. By the time I had been sitting there forty minutes, I became alarmed. I second-guessed my memory on where Steve had told me to sit. Maybe I was on the wrong bench. I'm the type who often stands in a line for days only to find out when my turn comes that I'm in the wrong line. The one I'm supposed to be in is in the next town.

Steve had told me the main parking lot was directly out the doors behind my bench, and he would be coming in from that lot. I hesitated to leave my spot to see if the parking lot was truly behind me. What if Steve came in from some other direction, and we missed each other? I needed to talk to someone.

Looking over at the couple slurping their interminable ice cream cones, I hesitantly said, "Excuse me. Could you tell me if the main parking lot is located behind us?"

With a long pause and a withering look of derision, the "gentleman" growled with a condescending grimace, "Ye-essss!"

I said, "Thank you." Then I studied him for a second, and as I did, a mischievous thought (perhaps it was a devilish thought) snaked into my mind. I added sweetly, "You see, this is an especially important evening for me. I'm about to meet someone I've never seen before. He's the father of my daughter."

All licking came to a frozen halt as their ice cream-smeared faces whiplashed in my direction. As if the God of the universe were orchestrating the timing of all this, a man then came through the doors from the parking lot behind me. I knew it had to be Steve. Our eyes met, we nodded at each other, and he hurriedly made his way toward me. I looked at him and then at the crabby couple woodenly staring at me. I thought, *I'm not done with you yet!*

I waited for Steve to get directly in front of me and then I leaped up, threw my arms around his neck, and breathlessly said, "Oh, Steve, it's wonderful to finally see you with the lights on!" Casting a triumphant look at the "fun" couple, who sat in stunned silence on the bench, their melting ice cream now dripping down their shirt sleeves, I thrust my arm through Steve's, and we made a quick exit.

Of course my comments and behavior required an explanation—to Steve at least. He started laughing long before I finished telling him everything . . . I really liked that. In fact, I really liked him.

I cherish all these meaningful and quirky memories . . . some bittersweet and some simple perks of cheer. On those days when I feel a bit discouraged or overwhelmed with my circumstances, I simply flash some of my favorite memories that I've converted into screen images and see yet again the stunned faces of my rude airport companions, Elias Gulah's plaid jacket and too-short striped pants, and Maude Amy's ostrich-feathered blue hat, ill-fitting brown coat, and white nurse's shoes.

Since the mind's storehouse is so vast, so too is the potential then for my mental videos. The poet William Wordsworth said memory can be called the "inward eye." One can actually see all that is stored in memory. Seeing and reliving those good memories can give me a giggle as well as a break from the circumstances that threaten to overwhelm me during a different time.

If this sounds at all appealing to you, try unfurling your own scroll of remembrances. Zero in on some quirky, encouraging, or just plain pleasant experiences that lightened some moments for you. Settle into a comfortable chair with a bag of popcorn and start those videos rolling. You may have such a good time you'll need another bag of popcorn!

10
Finding Forgiveness in Memory's Warehouse

*Bear with each other and forgive whatever grievances you may
have against one another. Forgive as the Lord forgave you.*

—Colossians 3:13

I giggle whenever my scroll of remembrance unfurls on
the story of my son, Jeff, who at the age of six was stealth-
ily working his way through a package of his favorite
mystic mint cookies just before dinnertime. He was sitting
cross-legged on the floor in the laundry room when I interrupted his stolen moment. Jumping to his feet, he handed
me the bag, told me he was just finishing, and thought he
would head on out the door to play. I told him I thought
he and I should have a bit of a discussion about the cookies before he went anywhere.

"I guess I should ask forgiveness, huh, Mama?"

Noting his cheerful face and remorseless tone of voice,
I said, "Well, only if you're sorry."

With initial confusion followed by relief, he offered this
logic: "Why should I be sorry? I love mystic mint cookies;
I love eating them. Being sorry would be just plain dumb!"

A Christian Requirement

Asking forgiveness or finding within ourselves the capacity to forgive others is a real cheer squelcher. As a Christian, the only way you could have missed hearing that we have to forgive is if you were somehow mistakenly left on a rock in Eden eating custard-filled chocolate eclairs by a fern-shrouded waterfall. To make the subject of forgiveness even more unpalatable, we have to forgive people who don't deserve it. Actually, what those people deserve are the many colorful punishments that a vengeful mind can put together in a matter of moments. But, no, we need to cease our creative imaginings and forgive them instead!

Sometimes the subject of forgiveness seems just plain dumb, which was Jeff's view of the mystic mint cookies. It seems dumb to have to forgive when someone has lied to us, cheated us, maligned us, abused us, or deceived us. Forgiveness for those persons simply goes against our emotional and logical sense of justice. Our more civilized selves know not to put sharp tacks on their driveway or send birthday cakes laced with arsenic. Though we might experience short-term pleasure in imagining such retribution, most of us refrain from taking overt retaliatory action. Perhaps we even congratulate ourselves for such restraint and smugly think that such control in itself is virtuous.

The part that is not dumb about forgiving people who have wounded us is that forgiving those who have wronged us restores our own cheer. Forgiving whomever inspired that bitterness and resentment brings wonderful release. Most of us are aware of the healing effects of forgiving those who have wounded us. But in spite of that knowledge, many of us continue to resist forgiving because of some misconceptions floating around about the subject. I'd like to talk about some of those hindrances, confining our discussion to the hurts that have been inflicted on us by others.

Forgiveness—and Distance

One of the misconceptions we might have about forgiveness is that, if we forgive, we have to "get back together" with that person. That very thought could send us racing to the airport for a one-way ticket to Antarctica.

We need to mentally separate the act of forgiveness and the act of reuniting. They are not the same. We can forgive our offender and still plan never to see that person again. He or she may even be toxic to us. To continue in a relationship with someone like that makes about as much sense as daily drinking a small glass of strychnine with our morning toast and then wondering why we're nauseous by noon. Forgiving the offender does not change the offender . . . it changes us. If the offender sincerely repents of his or her misdeeds, asks forgiveness, and then gives ample evidence of healthy, new behavior, reunion becomes a possibility.

When Ken and I were first married, we realized our apartment complex had

> *Forgiving the offender does not change the offender . . . it changes us.*

a newspaper thief. On some mornings our paper would be

in front of our door, but gradually, the paper was there less and less often. The newsboy assured us the delivery was being made. So Ken decided to lie in wait in an effort to catch whomever was making off with our paper.

Crouching below the window early one morning, when Ken heard approaching footsteps, he leaped to the front door and flung it open just in time to see our little, elderly neighbor, Mrs. Tollison, scoop up our paper. They both stared at each other in stunned silence—she at being caught and Ken at never suspecting Mrs. Tollison was a paper thief.

She burst into tears, handed the paper to Ken, and apologized profusely, saying she was so sorry and that she would never do that again. Ken took the paper, accepted her apology, woke me up, and said, "Marilyn, I disarmed the paper thief. We now can live in renewed security."

Several mornings later Ken had to leave our apartment early and in so doing caught a glimpse of Mrs. Tollison scooping up our neighbor's paper and scurrying down the stairs with it. Obviously, in spite of Mrs. Tollison's apology, her behavior did not change, which causes one then not to trust her expressions of remorse.

Actually, I later learned from our apartment owner that "sweet" Mrs. Tollison had to be watched on a regular basis. Apparently, she didn't mind walking into people's unlocked apartments during the day and taking whatever appealed to her. And what seemed to appeal to her most were gold jewelry and silver spoons!

When we forgive our offenders, we are not obligated to welcome those people back into our lives. (I kept my doors locked in spite of forgiving Mrs. Tollison.) Just because someone is forgiven does not guarantee that we will then welcome that person as a friend, spouse, or business partner. We can forgive as God enables us to do so but still realize our well-being might be jeopardized were we to reunite.

Forgiveness, Not Condoning

Another misconception we sometimes have is that forgiving someone's offense against us excuses the person's behavior. Forgiving does not excuse or condone . . . it simply forgives. The behavior remains the same: unacceptable, immoral, or even life-threatening.

In January 1984 the world was stunned to read that Pope John Paul II had gone to Rebibba Prison in Rome and offered his pardon to Mehmet Ali Agca, the twenty-six-year-old, Turkish-born terrorist who had attempted to kill the pontiff. The pope's forgiveness did not mean the young man's behavior was condoned; he was not released from jail as a result of the pope's pardon. His assault remained unacceptable and immoral; what changed was that he was forgiven by the pope. Mehmet Ali Agca still had to take responsibility for his behavior; there was no earthy justification for it. There is, however, divine forgiveness for it. The seeking and accepting of that divine forgiveness is Mehmet Ali Agca's responsibility.

Forgiving, Not Forgetting

Forgiving does not necessarily make the other person personally acceptable to us; forgiving does not condone the behavior of the other person; and forgiving does not mean forgetting the pain that individual inflicted on us. The concept of "forgive and forget" is something only God can do. We can't come anywhere near forgetting.

Most of us tote around a certain amount of guilt because the forgive-and-forget thing has never worked for us. We assume we really haven't forgiven because we know we haven't forgotten. But we haven't forgotten because of the way our brains work. That working is a wondrous study, and a brief understanding of the memory system might be liberating—just in case you've been giving yourself crabby messages about not forgetting.

Studies of the brain reveal that whatever seems important to us is stashed away in our long-term memory. Unimportant stimuli like mathematical formulas, directions for the VCR, and recipes for fricasseed liver are forgotten almost immediately, at least in my brain. The important stimuli, on the other hand, are held in our giant brain warehouses forever.

> *Forgive and forget is something only God can do.*

Unless an accident or disease damages our warehouses, those memories never disappear. Now that doesn't mean we can always access those memories; sometimes we have psychological resistance to remembering because recalling certain incidents would be too painful. The memory doesn't disappear, though; it's just lying low because that makes us feel safer.

The test of whether we have forgiven someone is not whether we remember the incident but in the attitudes and behaviors we exhibit. We know we have forgiven someone when we are no longer controlled by the pain and no longer doing a price check on cyanide. In other words, we remember the occurrence, but it no longer has power over our thinking and behavior.

Forgiving is better than forgetting, but God does both. Micah 7:18–19 describes God's style of forgiving:

> Where is another God like you, who pardons the sins of the survivors among his people? You cannot stay angry with your people, for you love to be merciful. Once again you will have compassion on us. You will tread our sins beneath your feet; you will throw them into the depths of the ocean! (TLB)

Don't you love that? God doesn't stay mad at us because He loves to show mercy and compassion. Instead, He stomps on our confessed sins and flings them into the ocean. What vivid and liberating images! And then He does what we can't do: "I, even I, am he who blots out your transgressions, for my own sake, and remembers your sins no more" (Isa. 43:25).

God's style of forgiveness serves as a model for us as we attempt to forgive with mercy

> *God stomps on our confessed sins and flings them into the ocean.*

and compassion; we don't need to worry about forgetting. The reality is we'll probably never close the drapes on those memories.

Choosing to Forgive

Okay, that sounds great. God has forgiven us, and now we are to forgive others. But what if we're not motivated to forgive? In fact, what if we aren't interested in forgiving? After all, there's a certain pleasant-unpleasant familiarity with our unforgiving attitude that might be missed were it removed. We've learned to live with it. We can also learn to walk with ingrown toenails, bunions, and one leg shorter than the other, but it isn't a cheerful walk. We manage to get around, all right, but not with much pleasure, and in some cases, not without calling attention to ourselves (depending on how much shorter that one leg is than the other).

Forgiving begins with our will; it is a choice. Something within our will must nudge us in the direction of forgiving. When Jeff was caught with his hand in the mystic mint cookie bag, nothing seemed to move him in the direction of seeing his behavior as requiring forgiveness. He knew he wasn't supposed to be eating cookies at 4:30 in the afternoon. Why else would he tuck himself in partial obscurity between the washer and dryer?

We have to recognize our wrong attitudes and behaviors, and then, with our will, decide to ask forgiveness for those attitudes based on the knowledge that it is the thing we're supposed to do whether we feel like it or not. As believers in Christ, who instructed us to love as He loves and forgive as He forgives, we really don't have an option here—unless, of course, we choose to live in disobedience and cheerlessness.

I suggested to Jeff that he pray and ask Jesus to help

him want to ask for forgiveness in eating the cookies. He finally decided that would probably be the only thing that would work for him because he still didn't see any logic in feeling sorry about what he had done. (He couldn't seem to separate his pleasure from the disobedience of breaking the late-cookie-eating rule.) Halfheartedly he prayed for an attitude of "being sorry," and halfheartedly he then asked for forgiveness.

The next day I heard him in his room telling his little sister, Beth, that being a Christian was probably pretty dumb. When she asked him why, he told her it meant you couldn't eat cookies whenever you wanted to. (*Way to go, Marilyn!*)

Sometimes we need to pray for the desire to forgive, for a holy nudge. But there are times when, in the absence of the nudge, we simply determine with our will to forgive. We invoke God's enabling strength, compassion, and power and humbly ask Him to do through us that which we are struggling to do and which, in our own strength, we know we can't. God honors our prayer of determination to forgive when it's based on our obedience to His Word to do so.

A Triple Reaffirmation of Love

Another way of forgiving goes beyond our mental determination. It is forgiving at a deeper level. I believe that bestowing forgiveness on this level more fully restores cheer because it more fully heals our original pain. Let me first give a biblical example of this type of forgiveness.

All four Gospels record Peter's denial of Jesus, but each includes slightly different details. Matthew and Mark record that Peter cursed and swore while Mark 14:72 says, "When Peter thought about it, he wept (NKJV)." Luke wrote, "The Lord turned and looked at Peter, . . . and he . . . wept bitterly" (22:61–62, NKJV). Luke also wrote that a fire was in the hall and Peter was seated by it. John went into even greater detail and wrote, "It was cold, and the servants and officials stood around a fire they had made to keep warm. Peter also was standing with them, warming himself" (18:18).

All this detail comes into play again in John 21 about a week after Jesus had shown Himself to His friends on the evening of resurrection day. The disciples had fished all night and weren't catching a thing. They were starting to come back to shore, cold and defeated. Then they saw a man standing on the beach who told them to throw their net from the other side of the boat. When they did, their net was so full of fish they couldn't even pull it back into the boat. The disciples then realized it was Jesus on the shore. He had fish cooking over the fire and invited His friends to join Him for breakfast.

After they had eaten and were comfortable, Jesus began to question Peter. "Do you love Me?" Jesus asked.

Peter had denied the Lord three times, standing by a fire while he warmed himself just a little over a week ago. Now Jesus was leading him to affirm his love three times, once again as he warmed himself by the fire. Three times Jesus asked the question, and Peter replied three times, "Yes, Lord, you know I love you."

Jesus' repeated question gave Peter an opportunity to relive what must have been an excruciating memory of betrayal. But, in the reliving, Jesus was literally there to provide His healing touch as well as to affirm His forgiveness of Peter.

For the rest of his life, Peter could have felt worthless and depressed by the memory of his denial. In all probability, he would have gone back to being a fisherman. Instead, Jesus, with His unconditional love for Peter, healed Peter's pain and *forgave* his denial. This enabled Peter to be filled with the Holy Spirit at Pentecost and to proclaim Jesus as Lord and Savior to the world.

What is so interesting to me about that morning barbecue is the reenactment of the three-time affirmation of love from Peter and the presence of a fire in both the denial scene and then in the forgiveness scene. It is this attention to detail that is another intriguing dimension of how our memories work. Research has shown that not only is an incident itself stored in the long-term warehouse but so also is the sensory memory attached to it: sights, sounds, and smells.

I can imagine how poignant it must have been for Peter to once again feel the chill in the air, to see the flames from the fire, and to smell the smoke curling from it. How overwhelmingly vivid that reenactment must have been for him! But it is this inclusion of as many senses as possible that helps pull up more deeply all

Jesus . . . healed Peter's pain and forgave *his denial.*

the warehoused pain so it can be relived and then healed through God's enabling forgiveness.

Returning to the Scene

I believe that to forgive more fully, we benefit by going back to the scene where the hurt originated, just as Jesus took Peter back. The comfort for our souls is that we don't go back alone. We don't have the benefit of Jesus' physical presence as Peter did, but we have His spiritual presence with us at all times.

If you find yourself drawn to this means of forgiving, you can invite Jesus into that hurting hollow that has never healed and from which you've possibly never even expressed a desire to forgive. May I suggest you find a quiet, private place where you will be free from interruption and distraction. Breathe deeply and slowly for a few minutes until you feel the inner "noise" begin to subside and you can concentrate more fully. Choose a verse that is especially meaningful to you that speaks of Jesus' unfailing, unconditional love for you. Say that verse aloud and insert your name in it. Quietly and reverently repeat the verse over and over until its divine truth penetrates into the depths of your soul.

Next, on the screen of your mind, begin to see the scene of your hurt . . . where you were . . . how old you were . . . what you were wearing. Be aware of sounds, colors, smells. Recall who was there . . . what he or she was wearing . . . note the expression on the face.

Now invite Jesus to come into that scene. If you wish, have Him hold your hand or gather you up into His arms. What we know beyond a shadow of a doubt is that He was there then, and He is there now. He is not bound by past or present.

In His presence and in His strength say to your offender, who cannot hurt you here, "I forgive you in Jesus' name. I forgive you for His sake. I forgive you for my sake."

Now see yourself and Jesus walk away from this scene. Thank Him for His sweet love for you, thank Him that He will never leave you, and thank Him that you do not need to live with the pain and hurt of the memory that has shriveled your soul, diminished your worth, and robbed you of your cheer. Thank Him that because of Him you are free to live your life without the controlling bitterness of unforgiveness; because of Him you are able to "be of good cheer."

11
When We Can't Change

O LORD, . . . I am weak. Heal me, for my body is sick, and I
am upset and disturbed. My mind is filled with apprehension
and with gloom. . . Come, O LORD, and make me well.
In your kindness save me.

—Psalm 6:2–4 (TLB)

Calvin, a lonely bachelor who felt his life could be enriched in some way other than marrying, decided to buy a parrot with whom he could occasionally engage in meaningful conversation. He made his way to a pet store and asked the owner for an especially talkative parrot. The owner said he had only one really verbal parrot but that he kept him in the back of the shop behind closed doors. Calvin was intrigued and insisted on buying the bird from the reluctant shopkeeper.

The parrot had been settled in his new cage for only a few moments when a stream of loud oaths and vile language began to pour forth from the bird's beak, causing Calvin to dash about madly slamming shut the doors and windows. He was horrified that such language should be heard coming from his apartment.

Calvin tried desperately to clean up the bird's language

but without success. These frequent and filthy diatribes made it impossible to have friends and family over, greatly curtailing Calvin's already impoverished social life.

During one especially offensive cursing episode, Calvin yanked the bird out of the cage, flung it in the freezer, and slammed the door. He heard it squawking, swearing, and thrashing about for a few minutes, and then suddenly, it became deathly quiet. Calvin waited a few more minutes before cautiously opening the freezer door.

To his surprise, the parrot stood there looking back at him. After an additional moment of silence, the parrot said, "Sir, I deeply regret my obscene language and utterly reprehensible behavior. I wish to apologize for the embarrassment I have caused you. Furthermore, I promise to never again speak in a manner that would bring shame upon your name. I hope to be a source of pleasure and good company for you in the future. I do wonder, sir, if you could graciously grant me one favor and answer a question that has hung heavily on my mind for the last few minutes."

Stunned, Calvin said, "Well . . . of course . . . what is it?"

"Sir," the parrot faltered, glancing around him at the contents of the freezer, "would you mind telling me what the chicken did?"

It Sounds So Easy . . .

Obviously, this parrot was a great candidate for behavior modification. Deciding he didn't like the possible consequences of his unacceptable behavior, he realized the wisdom of changing his ways. In essence, what we've been talking about throughout this book is changing our ways (not to be confused with those of the parrot) by changing our habits and attitudes, which will then produce our God-authored cheer. We have stressed that our ability to choose our mind habits is something over which we have control.

Though I believe that to be true for the majority of us, for some people, the message of "just choose" may have created guilt and possibly even despair. "If it were that simple," you might be saying, "don't you think I'd choose it? The reality is I can't . . . I have no mental, emotional, or physical stamina to just choose, and when you keep saying that, Marilyn, I want to slip you a good-for-one-visit coupon to see Dr. Jack Kevorkian."

Perhaps we should take up the subject of when and why it is sometimes difficult to "just choose." Let's begin by discussing physical challenges.

My daughter-in-law, Carla, is one of those exuberant, creative, fun-loving, and quirky (a prerequisite for becoming a Meberg) souls one can't help but love immediately. Before she married my son, Jeff, she was head of communications for Chuck Swindoll's "Insight for Living" radio ministry. She supervised the artistic layout for study guides, brochures, book jackets; planned cruises sponsored by the ministry, and worked on any other project that required a knowledge of people, art, or marketing.

Luci Swindoll, in one of her great revelations, decided few women were good enough for "her" Jeff Meberg, but Carla definitely qualified as worthy. So Luci set about plotting how she could get them together. When Luci was invited to be a speaker on a cruise Carla orchestrated, I was asked to be a part of the speaking team too. Luci made sure that Ken, Beth, and Jeff were also able to go.

Ken and I watched with utter delight as a relationship began to not only develop between Jeff and Carla but then to flourish into a budding romance. We were captivated with Carla's off-the-wall antics as well as her enthusiastic faith. Six months after the cruise, Jeff and Carla became engaged. (Luci was ecstatic—and so were Ken and I!)

Four months prior to the wedding, Carla was selected to travel to India as a member of a team of successful young American businesswomen. With characteristic enthusiasm, Carla returned from India touched by her experiences with the people and thrilled with new insights about the country. She also returned with a cough and a growing exhaustion that rest did not seem to assuage.

Jeff and Carla were married overlooking the Pacific Ocean on the grounds of the Ritz-Carlton Hotel in Laguna Niguel; it was one of the most beautiful weddings I've ever attended. (I supposed every mother of the bride or groom says that, but I assure you, in this case it was true!) The bride was also one of the most beautiful, but she also appeared to be one of the most exhausted people in attendance. In fact, Carla collapsed several days into the honeymoon and barely had the energy to walk. Many months and many tests later, she was diagnosed with tuberculosis as well as typhoid fever, both of which she contracted in India.

When You Don't Have a Choice

She was treated for those diseases, but her doctor (a female internist from India) told Carla and Jeff she feared Carla was carrying a number of other Third World viruses that were difficult to isolate for treatment. With all these diseases wreaking havoc in Carla's body, her immune system became greatly compromised, leaving her with chronic fatigue syndrome.

To watch Carla battle the vast array of symptoms that characterize CFS (profound and often prolonged fatigue, chronic low-grade fever, chills, night sweats, shortness of breath, irregular heartbeat, and sleep disturbance, to name a few) has been heart-wrenching. This once vibrant young woman has had to identify her physical limits and learn to operate within them; so too has Jeff in being her husband.

Carla and Jeff still do fun things. They have taken several cruises with friends, which allows Carla to rest but get in on the action when she's able. Thankfully, she still has flashes of those zany moments that are so endearing, and on occasion, she and Jeff dash out to see me in the desert.

Last weekend was one of those times. We loved lounging in the pool, fighting over who should get out of the pool to buy burgers at Carl's and arguing whether the blue raft was mine, Jeff's, or Carla's. Later that day Jeff read aloud the chapters of this book that tell about his grandfather's irrepressible zest for living and the option we all have to make those choices for our lives.

Very quietly Carla said, "I used to be a Jasper, but the

will to live that way is no longer an option for me. Sometimes people just don't have a choice. Are you going to say that, Marilyn?"

Yes, dear Carla, I'm going to say that. Sometimes people *don't* have a choice. Illness can at times be so debilitating the only choice for which we have enough energy is to will ourselves through the day. And sometimes even that requires more energy than we think we can muster. But even so, within the human spirit resides a seemingly indefatigable will to survive, to move forward, to hang on and not cave in.

In spite of the myriad of symptoms working against Carla, I have watched her determine to have at least some life beyond the four walls of her home. Though she can no longer work, she has enrolled in Westminster Seminary, where she is indulging her long-held craving to study theology. At times she has to rely on the benevolence of compassionate professors if she needs to drop a class or postpone a paper or take a final exam after the semester ends, but something in her propels her forward in spite of the many delays. Triumphantly, Jeff announced last weekend that Carla had received an A in her first Greek class. I'm able-bodied and healthy and can't imagine earning an A in a Greek class! Have you *seen* that alphabet?

The Life-Giving Word

Early in Carla's illness, when she couldn't get out of bed, even then something—actually, Someone—propelled her forward. It was that Someone about whom the psalmist wrote, "This is my comfort in my affliction, for Your word has given me life" (Ps. 119:50, NKJV). Lying in bed, Carla memorized Scripture. It gave her comfort and consolation; it revived her and gave her life.

That is not to say she did not succumb at times to indescribable grief at the unexpected stripping away of her health and stamina. To contemplate her future as a near invalid instead of a fully functioning and contributing individual has been devastating. Nevertheless, Carla knew she had a choice in how she responded to her illness. She could rail against God and become bitter, or she could memorize Scripture and become spiritually stronger. Those were her choices. Rising up and living the active life she had enjoyed before was not. Unless one is dead or has no mind, there are still choices to be made despite debilitating illness.

Three-Part Personhood

Another arena in which many persons struggle and think they can't just choose to change their attitudes is when they have difficulties with their mental and emotional health. Statistics state that approximately one out of twenty persons in the United States experiences severe depression. That means a vast number of people do not have the capacity to will themselves into a place of emotional well-being.

Since I have spent a number of years working in the mental health profession, I have enormous compassion for emotional suffering. What especially breaks my heart is remembering the Christians who came into my office feeling defeated because they viewed their emotional struggles as an indication of a lack of faith and trust in God. "If I prayed more, believed more, trusted more, I'd feel better," they would say. Or they would speculate, "Maybe I'm not even a Christian. If I were, I could get a grip. Something must be hopelessly wrong with my faith."

I would like to share a liberating truth from Scripture that I hope will give encouragement to those who feel that emotional or mental turmoil is always the result of faulty faith. We are three-part persons: body, spirit, and soul. As we understand what each part plays in our personhood, we can be freed from assigning our difficulties to inadequate faith.

But first, let me explain how our being is made up of three parts.

Genesis 2:7 states, "And the LORD God formed man of the dust of the ground [body], and breathed into his nostrils the breath of life [spirit]; and man became a living soul" (KJV).

And remember that the Word of God can divide or distinguish the soul from the spirit (see Heb. 4:12).

Finally, 1 Thessalonians 5:23 tells us, "I pray God your whole spirit and soul and body be preserved blameless unto the coming of our Lord Jesus Christ" (KJV).

Now to understand more fully the significance of these verses and their references to our three-part persons, let's talk about each designation. We all know what the body is, but it's important to remember that it is innocent of any wrongdoing. It simply houses our spirit and soul. The problems of the body are pretty obvious: aches, pains, injuries, and diseases, none of which is the body's fault.

If my car suddenly stops in the middle of the freeway because it's out of gas, I can hardly blame the car and determine to trade it in once I push it out of the fast lane. Because the car has no gas is not its fault . . . it's mine. The body, like the car, is dependent on conscientious maintenance.

The spirit is that part of us made in what Scripture calls the "image" of God (see Gen. 1:26–27; 5:3; 9:6). He gives us a spiritual nature that is made like Him. It can respond to Him and have a relationship with Him. That relationship is made possible when we receive Christ as Savior. He comes into our interior beings, our spirits, and we become "new creations" (see 2 Cor. 5:17); God's Spirit then is joined to our spirit. That He is joined forever to our spirits is wonderful!

Equally fantastic and perhaps even more encouraging is our understanding of the soul. The soul is our psychological being, that place where our emotions, intellect, and desires exist. The Greek word for soul is *psyche*. It is in our souls, or psyches, that we experience feelings like isolation, abandonment, betrayal, and other soul-eroding emotions. It is in our souls, then, in which we experience mental and emotional distress. When we remember God has connected Himself to our spirit at the point of conversion, that means no matter how turbulent our souls may be, God has not nor will He ever disconnect from our spirit, no matter what we feel.

Do you remember Romans 7:15–16, in which Paul talked about feeling so frustrated with himself? "I don't understand myself at all, for I really want to do what is right, but I can't. . . . I know perfectly well that what I am doing is wrong" (TLB). Was Paul struggling with his *spirit* here? Absolutely not. He was struggling with his soul. As long as you and I are on this earth we're going to struggle with our souls.

The soul also houses our will, our mental determinations. Sometimes we feel as if we're in a war zone because, like Paul, we know what we ought to do, but we don't will ourselves to do it. That's why Paul wrote in Philippians 2:13, "For it is God who works in you to will and to act according to his good purpose." It is in our wills, our souls, that God is continually working to conform us to Christ's image. It is in our wills, our souls, that God's refining fire works on us to do His will.

> ♡ *It is in our wills, our souls, that God's refining fire works on us to do His will.*

As we understand the soul's function, we realize we are not substandard, inadequate Christians when we fall victim to its maladies. When we suffer from mental and emotional distress, God is still living within us, still connected to our spirit.

Beware the Accuser!

Incidentally, it might be wise to remember that Satan is the enemy of our souls; the soul is the devil's playground. It is his voice that whispers messages to discourage us, diminish us, and condemn us. It's his voice that suggests God could never forgive us, stick by us, or love us. It is his voice that tells us we aren't good enough, spiritual enough, or worthy enough to receive salvation. And it is His voice that accuses us of inadequate faith and imperfect mental health. God calls him an "accuser" (Rev. 12:10), and that very word is our cue to recognize when Satan is having a heyday in our souls. The Holy Spirit never accuses. Instead, He woos us, He wins us, and He loves us to behave better and to commit ourselves more deeply to Him. When we feel unworthy and unable, we've succumbed to the enemy's accusing voice. He never gives up his attacks on the soul.

At no time is the accuser's voice louder than when we fall prey to major depression. The defenses against these attacks can become so depleted that the anguished soul can no longer fight back. Severe depression settles in then, filling every nook and cranny of our beings with what feels like an impenetrable fog of hopelessness.

One of my dear friends, whom I will call Jane, lost her mother to cancer when Jane was fourteen. Being the oldest of four girls, Jane leaped in to help fill the void for her devastated and emotionally fragile pastor-father.

She cooked, cleaned, mothered her three sisters, and did everything in her power to reestablish the shattered order of their home. The church members were so concerned with their pastor's depth of grieving, no one seemed to be aware of the young teenager's valiant efforts to hold everyone and everything together.

Years later, Jane graduated from high school with top honors and an all-tuition-paid scholarship to a Christian college several states away. The father, sisters, and church members worried how the family would manage without Jane.

Several months into her freshman year, Jane began to awaken each morning around 2 A.M. with a wildly palpitating heart accompanied by a sense of pervasive fear and dread. Frightened and confused by these early-morning feelings of panic, Jane, in a desperate attempt to rid her mind of the oppressive fear that threatened to envelop her, worked even harder during the day. She taught her dormitory Bible study each week, volunteered to read for three blind students, and increased her own study time.

Contrary to what she hoped to accomplish, her efforts resulted in more episodes of early-morning panic. She cried out to God to please help her, to calm her, to soothe her, to take away the awful fear and dread, and to give her victory. Her desperate prayers appeared to fall on deaf ears.

Jane couldn't understand God's indifference to her pleas. What had she done to displease him? She had tried so hard to do everything right. While she pleaded with God to show her what she needed to do differently, she became more panicked and ultimately unable to function.

Shortly before Christmas Jane was admitted to a psychiatric hospital for clinical depression. She begged her doctor not to tell her father where she was. "He'll never be able to handle it. Please, please don't tell him. He isn't strong enough."

However, the doctor had to tell the father, and sure enough, he wasn't able to handle it. Various members of the church stepped in to cook, clean, and tend to the three younger girls as well as to care for the now bedridden father.

Years later, as Jane described this experience to me, she said the most devastating element of all was her sense of utter failure as a Christian. She was sure, for reasons she could not fathom, that God had removed Himself from her because she was spiritually inadequate and displeasing to Him.

The reality was, she was not a failure as a Christian. She was, instead, one whose soul needed tending and mending. God was there for that with the same meticulous love and attention to her healing process as He had bestowed on the miraculous creation of the world and all that is in it. Nothing about us is incidental to God. Nothing about us diverts His attention from our well-being. And nothing stems the flow of His compassion.

Through Christian counseling, Jane gradually began to understand the anguished state of her soul. When her mother died, she had not allowed herself to grieve that enormous loss. In fact, she had not even allowed herself to cry. Instead, in an effort to rescue her father and sisters from their grief responses, she sacrificed her own. She tried to step into her mother's shoes and become the caretaker, not only of her sisters, but also of her father.

♡Nothing about us is incidental to God.

Jane didn't date throughout high school because her home responsibilities were too great. She studied long and hard, knowing her good grades would have pleased her mother, and she hoped they would help her dad. Through it all, Jane, the little fourteen-year-old girl who had lost her mom, actually lost her dad as well. That meant no one was there to parent Jane. Her personhood, with all its fourteen-year-old pain and confusion, was simply erased, and she became whatever was needed for everyone else. Jane disappeared.

Under the care of a professional Christian counselor, Jane explored the wounds she had experienced, and as she did so, God's graciousness became increasingly sweet to her. She realized that, had she not experienced her "break period," she would never have understood how valuable she is to God as an individual. She gradually came to understand that she was created to have her own joys and sorrows (not someone else's), and she was created to express those feelings. We are to bear one another's burdens but not to the exclusion of our own. Though she dearly loved her father, it was not the job of a little girl to be her father's strength. He was supposed to be that for her.

She also experienced the release that came from expressing the tears, pain, and sorrow of finally grieving the excruciating loss of her mother. She learned not only that it was okay to cry but that it was also necessary. God created tears as a healthy and even mandatory release for the toxins that accumulate in the body. (Tears that come from sorrow have a different chemical composition than tears that come from joy. There are no toxins in joy tears, only in grieving tears.)

Jane returned to school for the spring semester with a new perspective about herself, about God, and about the life He had given her. She learned that, yes indeed, life has times of trials and sorrows, but she also learned how dearly she was loved and that she had become an overcomer because of the One who loved her. And that realization brought her a new source of cheer.

Choosing to Seek Help

Many of us have souls like Jane's. They are lacerated with wounds from the past and the present. We've tried to pray our way through the pain, and yet, for reasons known only to God, the anguish remains. That doesn't mean God has left; He never leaves. Remember, He is the God of our souls as well as of our spirits. Perhaps He means for us to take a closer look at that anguish so He might fully heal us of whatever residue is keeping us immobilized and without victory. The person whose pain is so deep she feels she may be losing her mind or has no impetus to live may need to choose a Christian mental health professional to help her work through those issues.

Then she may make an additional choice that can also be a tremendous help. She can discuss with her mental health professional the possibility of using medication to help her overcome the problem. Drugs like Prozac, Zoloft, and Paxil have been remarkably successful in helping severely depressed persons. Those drugs use a flouxetine compound that helps the body increase its levels of serotonin, the neurotransmitter that has been linked with feelings of well-being. Depressed persons typically have low levels of serotonin available to their brain cells because of its rapid absorption by other cells throughout the body.

Sometimes Christians have difficulty allowing themselves to take medications for severe depression because they fear they are relying on a drug for emotional and psychological help rather than on God. In my view, that logic would dictate telling a diabetic to simply trust God more rather than take insulin. Or if I were a candidate for a root canal and using that same logic, I would refuse Novocain and instead pray fervently during the drilling and gouging of my teeth and gums. Or how about my hysterectomy? Should I tell my surgeon that instead of an anesthetic I'm going to sing hymns and believe in the God of miracles, who will grant a painless removal of my precious organs? None of that thinking makes sense to me.

One should be cautious, of course, about agreeing to use drugs for the reestablishing of emotional well-being. If a "feel-better" drug is used to treat mild depression or to simply enhance performance, that, in my view, is a mistake.

> *Sometimes Christians . . . fear they are relying on a drug for emotional and psychological help rather than on God.*

If we treat everything with a pill, we won't learn the real causes of the depression and anxiety that are plaguing the soul. It is crucial to understand the emotional issues that are dictating a hurting person's behaviors and determining her level of depression, and a Christian mental health professional is trained to help clients sort through those issues and then consider whether medication is a suitable choice.

Sometimes drugs are *not* the right choice because the hurting person simply needs to experience the pain. In some situations a pill would short-circuit the necessary growth, development, and character-building that accompany the hurt. These are the times when the task may well be to look at that wad of turmoil and determine there is no way around it and no way over it. There is only one choice at that point, and it is simply to go through it. The encouraging connotation of the word *through* in this scenario is that there is a beginning, a middle, and an end to the painful experience.

No quick and easy answers exist for the question of whether to take medications to treat emotional problems. But simple logic says if the will to live no longer exists, medication is needed! Or if someone has insufficient emotional energy to look at the pain that has seeped to the surface of her soul, then, she too needs medication. Generally, medication can be viewed as an emergency procedure that is necessary to ensure one's safety and to enable her to successfully work through the issues that have compounded her wounds. I thank God for those medical options.

Boundless Love without Prejudice

This chapter was written for the many persons who, because of physical illness or emotional difficulties, feel at times they simply can't muster the energy to will themselves into a more positive, cheer-producing attitude. What I'd like to leave with all of you, no matter what frailties or infirmities arise to challenge you, is that the love of God has no limits, no boundaries, and no prejudices. No matter who you are, where you are, or where you've been, He loves you. He holds you; He carries you; He remains with you at all times whether or not you feel Him beside you in the Valley of the Shadow.

In the words of Hannah Whitehall Smith,

"Put together all the tenderest love you know, the deepest you have ever felt and the strongest that has ever been poured out upon you, and heap upon it all the love of all the loving human hearts in the world, and then multiply it by infinity, and you will begin, perhaps, to have some faint glimpse of the love God has for you."

12
Toppled Over

*How we thank you, Lord! Your mighty miracles give proof
that you care.*

—Psalm 75:1

There's something about penguins. Maybe it's their short
legs and awkward walk; maybe it's their tidy tuxedo jackets; maybe it's their quirky ways. Whatever it is, penguins
charm me into a state of cheer, and I've had a lifelong love
of them. In fact, the first year Ken and I were married I
taught third grade, and one of my class's major science
projects was to study penguins.

One aspect of penguins that fascinated my group of
eight-year-olds, as well as their teacher, was the emperor
penguins' nesting habits. The female penguin briefly leaves
the ocean at the start of the Antarctic autumn, waddles up,
and lays an egg on the bare ice. She immediately returns to
the water.

The male takes over the job of keeping the egg warm
until it hatches. He rolls the egg onto his feet and covers it
with the lower part of his belly, which has several rolls of
fat. (A kind of built-in afghan.)

Carrying the egg on his feet, the male trundles into a

large group of other males, who are also on egg duty, and they all form a huddle. (Can't you just see that?) For two months they stand in a tight circle to keep each other and their eggs warm. For two months they do not eat. When the chick hatches, the female returns and takes over the mothering duties. The male heads for the water for food for himself as well as for the baby and Mom.

God's Delight in His Creation

I'm filled with wonder and cheer at the thought of how delightfully God has created penguins. They charm me and inspire me spiritually. They are waddling little over-comers who because of a God-created system survive Earth's harshest environment, living out their quirky lives with efficiency as well as organization. What's the source of their overcoming abilities? God. Plain, simple, and pro-found.

I love that Jesus made references to the birds of the air and the flowers of the field as objects of His loving care. In the divine mind, all creation is valued and provided for. In fact, Jesus even suggested we look to nature to note cre-ation's God-given ability to function, perform, and overcome, and then to be encouraged and cheered that His commitment to meeting our needs is even greater. What is equally inspiring to me is that God takes obvious delight in His creation. (You have to admit, hatching an egg on the toe of a penguin is zany!)

God's delight in us is expressed frequently in Scripture. For example, Psalm 18:19 states, "He brought me out into a spacious place; he rescued me because he delighted in me." It's mind-boggling to most of us that the God of the universe actually delights in us, but Scripture says He does.

If John 16:33 is a divine formula for cheerful living, we see that Jesus warned us we would experience bad stuff as long as we were on the earth. But in spite of all that, He says we can be cheerful because He has "overcome the world." The understanding of that last phrase is crucial to finding cheer in the midst of the "stuff." I think we first have to underscore the tremendous love and delight God feels for us before we even begin to grasp the magnitude of what He overcame on the cross. His love sent Jesus to the cross; knowing He delights in us allows us to feel secure about who we are and Whose we are.

> *Knowing He delights in us allows us to feel secure about who we are and Whose we are.*

We can't find cheer, as we've mentioned before, if we don't know Jesus as Savior. But when we do know Him, by virtue of His Spirit being linked to ours, we have access to His overcoming power for absolutely every trial that touches our lives.

To find cheer, we also must internalize the vast depth of God's love. How few of us really grasp that truth. We talk it, we quote it, we remind each other about it, but do we know it? I'll have to say in all candor, I struggle daily with my inability to comprehend God's boundless, unconditional, and even relentless love for me.

However, I don't think it's possible to be a cheerful overcomer without the sure foundation of knowing God loves me exactly as I am once I have received forgiveness for sin. I can't do anything to win Him, impress Him, or further convince Him I am worthy of His love and delight. That has already been done. Jesus did that on the cross. He made me perfectly and wholly acceptable to God—an impossible task on my own. That seems to be a truth that is difficult to internalize consistently.

Really Feeling God's Commitment

Barbara Johnson discovered a method that has helped me feel the depth of God's love for me. As she was flying home from one of our Joyful Journey conferences, she began to read an artistically created set of bound cards someone had handed to her at the conference. In calligraphy, Barbara's name had been inserted in various places in selected readings and paraphrases of Scripture that spoke of love and hope.

As Barbara read, she was overwhelmed to see her name in bold, black print in the center of these divine promises. She cried as she read them. When she arrived in California, she contacted Le Ann Weiss, the founder of the Encouragement Company, which specializes in these personalized Scripture packets, and ordered them for all of us on the speakers team. As we read our personal packets, each of us experienced the same tenderness and tears Barbara did when she opened hers.

I have pondered for some weeks why these cards should elicit such emotional responses. All the scriptures used are familiar; the thoughts are not new. But I realized that, at least for myself, I felt a powerful jolt from these scriptures when I saw *my name* included within each one in bold print. It was as if a new translation of the Bible had been written especially from God to me. I dare say that all of us who have responded with such deep feelings are reminded of what we thought we knew.

Let me share a few of those personalized verses with you. While your name doesn't appear in print here, try imagining it inserted where mine is and feel the effect of such personalized Scripture.

Remember, Marilyn, I AM FOR YOU! Who can be against you?

In all things, you are more than a victorious conqueror through Me!

Be convinced that nothing can stop Me from loving you . . .

Not death or life, angels or demons, current circumstances, or anything in your past or future!

Absolutely nothing or no one in all of the entire world can separate you from My totally awesome, unconditional and indescribable love for you!

Love,
Your God of Victory
Romans 8:37–39

P.S. Remember, I will never leave you or abandon you! Don't be afraid because I am your helper! Hebrews 13:5–6

Marilyn,

Catch a glimpse of my incredible and indescribable love for you.

I pray that you, being rooted and established in LOVE, may have power to grasp how wide and long and high and deep is My totally unconditional love for You! My love for you totally surpasses all human knowledge of love.

Everlasting Love,

Jesus

Ephesians 3:17–19

God is personal. He knows me, loves me, and has made a huge commitment to me. It's amazing how frequently that truth eludes me. Many of us struggle with that concept, so I am indebted to Dr. Charles Stanley for a story about learning to feel safe and loved. He tells it in his book *The Reason for My Hope.*

Buddy was a four-year-old foster child who had been severely abused. When he was placed in yet another foster home, the mother of that home was heartbroken as she watched this little fellow become terrified and frantic if he were approached. It was impossible to get near him without his yelling, screaming, and running wildly around the house.

One day, the foster mother decided she would do everything in her power to alleviate the child's fears. She went into Buddy's room and closed the door behind her.

Buddy panicked and began to run frantically around the room, screaming as loudly as he could while the foster mother sat calmly in a chair.

Over and over again she said, "Buddy, I love you. I'm not going to hurt you. I love you. I'm not going to hurt you."

Ultimately little Buddy collapsed in a corner in exhaustion. The mother still did not move but merely repeated, "Buddy, I love you. I'm not going to hurt you. I love you. I'm not going to hurt you."

When Buddy saw she had not moved from the chair, he uncurled from his cowering position, sat up, and stared at her. She then got up and left the room, still repeating, "Buddy, I love you. I'm not going to hurt you. I love you!"

The foster mother repeated this for two more days. Each day Buddy went through the same routine of screaming and running but for shorter periods of time. On the fourth day, the foster mother took a large doll into the room with her and cuddled it as she sat in the chair repeating the words, "Buddy, I love you. I'm not going to hurt you." She added, "Would you like to come and sit with my doll and me?"

By the seventh day little Buddy ventured toward the mother and the doll and allowed himself to be picked up. He was stiff and hesitant but did not resist the mother's stroking of his hair and talking gently to him. By the tenth day he finally relaxed in her arms, and she rocked him to sleep.

Though the majority of us have not had the abuse Buddy experienced the first four years of his life, I wonder how many of us still stare disbelieving from the corner of our hearts, afraid to venture forward to receive God's love. It's too good to be true, too big to be trusted, too foreign to be understood. Yet He softly says, "I love you. I'm not going to hurt you. I love you."

Studying Jesus, the Human Face of God

We know that God is tender and compassionate toward us because that was the response Jesus gave to people when He was on earth. Jesus is the human face of God. To know God's responses, we study those of Jesus.

For example, Matthew 9:36 says, "When he saw the crowds, he had compassion on them, because they were harassed and helpless, like sheep without a shepherd." Isaiah 40:11 states, "He tends his flock like a shepherd; He gathers the lambs in his arms and carries them close to his heart; he gently leads those that have young."

God is gently, lovingly, calling our names and inviting us to venture toward Him, inviting us not to be afraid. He is not going to hurt us.

If your need right now is to overcome a difficult situation such as making it through the pain and anxiety of divorce, it's unlikely you can tap into God's overcoming power if you aren't convinced He is for you and not against you. If your overcoming need is to have the strength and wisdom to deal with your kids, who have turned their backs on God and on the family, that overcoming power has to be viewed as part of your family inheritance from the God who cares even more for your children than you do. If your overcoming need has to do with the devastation that comes from a cancer diagnosis or some other debilitating disease, you have to know that God's love for you will never leave you as you begin to walk a path you never expected to make your way down. His love guarantees you won't walk it alone.

We need to stop our panicked running around the room, crawl into the loving arms of our Father, and let Him rock us until we find quietness and peace. Without the confidence we are loved, we won't find ways to overcome; nor will we find reasons to have a heart full of cheer.

Holding On to God's Steadfast Love

How do we deepen our experience of knowing God's love? Let me share three steps that help me hang on to the steadfast love that will not let me go. To begin with, personalizing Scripture, as we've discussed several times, is a powerful tool. It transforms *God's Word* into *God's Word especially designed for me.* For years I have read Scripture and inserted my name in the place of the personal pronouns. But after receiving the calligraphic cards from Barbara, I realized I needed to add a step and *write* my name into the verses rather than just *read* my name there.I need to see it, and see it often. I set those personalized cards around the house, car, or office where I constantly will encounter them. As I read the cards aloud, I'm involving the senses of sight and sound. The more of my senses I can involve, the greater the impact on my psyche (or soul).

Let's take some verses in Isaiah, which are wonderfully

nurturing, and personalize them. Isaiah 43:1 would read, "Fear not, Marilyn, for I have redeemed you; I have summoned you by name; you, Marilyn, are mine."

And Isaiah 54:10 would read, "'Though the mountains be shaken and the hills be removed, yet my unfailing love for you, Marilyn, will not be shaken nor my covenant of peace be removed,' says the LORD, who has compassion on you, Marilyn."

Scores of verses attest to God's love. Choose those that are especially meaningful to you, personalize them, and spread them around your environment.

The second step is to memorize these verses. Memorize them with your name in them. Say them to yourself so that even when you can't see them, you have them imprinted in your mind and soul. That makes them accessible anywhere, anytime.

Finally, practice God's presence. What does that really mean? I am a very new pilgrim on this path, and though I find it difficult to do well and am not qualified to talk about it at great length, let me tell you what this step means to me. To practice the presence of God means I think about God and acknowledge that He is always within me, even when I feel the least aware of His presence.

This requires effort on my part far beyond writing my name in Scripture and then memorizing it. This step requires serious discipline. As C. S. Lewis wrote in *Mere Christianity*:

That is why the real problem of the Christian life comes where people do not usually look for it. It comes the very moment you wake up each morning. All your wishes and hopes for the day rush at you like wild animals. And the first job each morning consists in shoving them all back: in listening to that other voice, taking that other point of view, letting that other larger, stronger, quieter life come flowing in. And so on, all day. . . .

We can do it only for moments at first. But from those moments the new sort of life will be spreading through our systems because now we are letting Him work at the right part of us. (*Mere Christianity*, Macmillan, 1978, 167)

I love Lewis's personifying our wishes and hopes for the day as wild animals that charge in and simply take over. That is so true of my experience. Yet as I purpose to practice God's presence, sometimes by simply saying His name, "Jesus," over and over, then I know He is within me, not way "out there" in cosmic space but indwelling me and my earthly environment.

> *Who in your lifetime . . . will ever be so utterly in love with you? Only God!*

I have learned that those animals can be tamed and corralled. The Spirit that indwells me also enables me to fix my mind on Him and to claim His literal presence in the room, car, office, or wherever. The more I am aware of His presence, the greater my joy and my cheer, even in the middle of the stuff life keeps handing me. I encourage you to practice His presence as well.

God's Joyous Love

I hope I have communicated in this book that when I allow the love of God to redeem me, hold me, and overcome the world for me, I will have learned what Jesus meant when He said, "Be of good cheer." I will have learned it is possible to walk through life, no matter what or whom I meet on the road, and know I can still be of good cheer. How? Why? Because He lives within me, and He is an overcomer. And because of His indwelling presence, so too am I.

All of these thoughts bring me to my all-time favorite, cheerful penguin story, which was sent to me through the Internet. As a result, I can't document it accurately, but I believe it appeared originally in the Audubon Society's magazine.

Bored Royal Air Force pilots stationed on the Falkland Islands devised what they thought was a wonderful game. Noting that the local penguins seemed fascinated by airplanes, the pilots searched out a beach where the greatest congregation of birds gathered. Then the pilots flew their planes slowly along the water's edge as nearly ten thousand penguins turned their heads in unison, watching the planes go by. When the pilots turned around to fly back, the birds turned their heads in the opposite direction, like spectators at a slow-motion tennis match. To give the penguins a little variety, the pilots flew out to sea, turned around, and flew over the top of the penguin colony. Once again, in unison, heads went up, up, up, until all ten thousand penguins toppled softly onto their backs.

The simple zest for life that these darling, bowled-over birds personify is also expressed in my heart as I am reminded of God's presence within me as stated in Zephaniah 3:16–18.

Cheer up, don't be afraid. For the LORD your God has arrived to live among you. He is a mighty Savior. He will give you victory. He will rejoice over you in great gladness; he will love you and not accuse you." Is that a joyous choir I hear? No, it is the LORD himself exulting over you in happy song (TLB).

Can you imagine God's delight in us is so genuine, so spontaneous, so spirited that He exults over us by singing happy songs? Can you imagine that He not only lives among us (within us) and promises to give us victory, but also that He rejoices over us in great gladness? Who in your lifetime—past, present, or future—has ever been or will ever be so utterly in love with you?

Only God! Plain, simple, profound. That realization is enough to cause me to look up, up, up, and topple over with cheer-inducing, heartfelt gratitude.

So come on! Grab your robe and join the joyous choir. There's a lot more living, loving, and laughing to do. Sure, there's plenty of stuff in this world to steal your joy. But remember, you have Jesus, the Overcomer. You have a choice. You can choose cheer over fear. And after all is said and done, wouldn't you rather be laughing?